The End of a Childhood

BY

Patrick G. Davis

Bloomington, IN

authorHOUSE™

Milton Keynes, UK

AuthorHouse™
1663 Liberty Drive, Suite 200
Bloomington, IN 47403
www.authorhouse.com
Phone: 1-800-839-8640

AuthorHouse™ UK Ltd.
500 Avebury Boulevard
Central Milton Keynes, MK9 2BE
www.authorhouse.co.uk
Phone: 08001974150

First published by AuthorHouse 5/5/2006

ISBN: 1-4259-2770-X (sc)

Printed in the United States of America
Bloomington, Indiana

This book is printed on acid-free paper.

Edited by Ann Gladem

*To my brothers and sisters and the people
that have inspired me to take my writings further.
Thanks Mom and Dad, I know you are always watching over
us.*

*~ Memory in the form of words is a gift from God that time can
not destroy ~*

Introduction

History has always been a favorite subject of mine. I figure unless I know someone's history I will never truly know who they are. Now if you looked back at the history of 1974, you would find some interesting facts. The Watergate break in caused President Nixon to resign, *People Magazine* began publication, Hank Aaron broke Babe Ruth's home run record, and the one hundred ten story World Trade Center, the tallest building at that time, opened in New York City. But those events would happen months down the road from where this story starts. Whether the history is good or bad, the fact is, it makes us remember. This story is not about anyone famous. It's about the small events that happened in my life and some of the people that were involved with them.

Ultimately, most of us can flag a certain day or time when we realize our childhood is over. I never realized how special my younger years were until that happened. As years pass, we have a tendency to only remember certain highlights of our childhood. Fortunately for me, I have so many memories, paper couldn't hold them all. A small city in Wisconsin along with the family and friends that surrounded my life contributed to the many memories worth writing about.

1

I studied the map long enough to memorize the route. I finally knew the best way to get to our destination, LaCrosse, Wisconsin. The cold January of 1974 found me at the age of eighteen and the third son in our family attempting college. Tomorrow, Mom and my youngest sister Mary will drive me to a place where all my past is behind me and my future will begin without any familiarity.

The family's black suitcase with the one broken latch was packed with all my important possessions. Mom kissed me and said softly, "Goodnight, honey." I went up the steps two at a time like I did many times. As I lay in bed, I went over the trek in my head down to the last detail. The last thing I wanted to do was get lost.

The smell of bacon, toast, fried potatoes, and coffee was my alarm clock. All the threats in the world couldn't roust me out of bed, but the grand aroma of breakfast was enough to make me throw the covers off my warm body. I sat on my bedside and looked out the window to see the leafless trees. It brought me back to a time when I was younger and the weather was warmer...

Eleven Years Earlier...

I opened my eyes and stared out of the screen window that was directly in front of me. My bed was eye level to the window sill, and I could see the sun landing on the roof of the house I grew up in. It was an older two-story home that was pushing the century mark. It made a comfortable pad for me and my five brothers and sisters. My eyes were just coming into focus when I saw the willow trees that my dad had planted in our backyard.

Their yellow branches were swaying in the slight breeze. The background was a light-blue sky. It was picturesque; almost puzzle like with all the wispy branches reaching for the earth. Being on the second floor, I noticed a small commotion occurring beneath me as I leaned and pressed my head against the screen. I could see our cat, Pierre, pouncing on something that wasn't visible from where I was. She was ribs deep in the Snow on the Mountain flowers. The green and white plants were overtaking the foundation of our home, and I could see only her gray tail sticking out of the plush vegetation. Her snakelike tail was snapping back and forth like a whip. She probably had another grasshopper. Pierre had a taste for them. She occasionally pranced in the house with one in her mouth and sometimes let them go, half alive to the dislike of my mother. It was common practice to look at Pierre's mouth as she scurried through the door because she learned to conceal them quite well.

It was then, when the realization finally hit me. It was a feeling that matched only a few things in life. It was the first day of summer vacation, ranking right up there with

Christmas and my birthday. If I had to choose between the three, I think summer vacation was the best. The euphoric feeling of total freedom made me smile. The idea of not having to go to school and being able to play baseball all summer was my idea of heaven. I could smell the fresh-cut grass as the warmth of the long-awaited summer reflected off the shingles. I closed my eyes wanting to take this memory in and lock it in my mind forever. Nothing in life compares to this. Three months of playing baseball, fishing, swimming, and the A & W Root Beer stand. I opened my eyes with a grin on my face that said *Life is good!*

I slid out of bed and peered across the room. I noticed my younger brother Eddie was still asleep. Last night we stayed up a little later than most nights. We always talked before bed, but the topic of summer vacation was almost too good to let rest. Eddie had a strong resemblance to Opie Taylor from *The Andy Griffith Show.* His blankets were balled around his belly, and his head was covered with his pillow. His legs were totally exposed, sticking out from the heap of cloth resembling blankets and sheets.

His bedding was totaled, probably due to his evening trip to the kitchen. Eddie had a tendency to sleep walk; occasionally, he would even talk while sleep walking too. More often than not, the words he spoke made little sense. We would always kid him about it the next day. One evening he plowed downstairs with that look in his eye. My mom was sitting at the dining room table as she saw him coming. Her only response was, "Uh oh." We knew we were in for some good stuff.

With almost a frightened look on his face, Eddie looked directly at me and said, "Where's Pat?"

My mom tried to hide a snicker as she stood up. "Eddie, Pat's right here," she said as she put her hand on my shoulder.

That answer wasn't good enough for Eddie. He asked with more urgency, "Where's Pat?"

We couldn't help laughing. I said, "I'm right here, Eddie." Mom had seen enough. She took Eddie by the arm and took him back upstairs to bed.

As she climbed the stairs, she looked over her shoulder and said, "Wait until we tell him about this in the morning." This story would go right along with the rest of them. Eddie would laugh with all of us as we would reenact the whole scene. Eddie's normal travels, when there was no one there to talk to, usually consisted of sixteen steps to the lower level of the house and then straight to the kitchen, where he would consume a half a box of cereal. If he was too tired to make the trip back upstairs, he would crash on the couch, or in the winter time, on the floor register. The soft warm heat flowing from the floor register was a great comfort in the winter. It wasn't uncommon to see Eddie or occasionally anybody else taking that position. Usually it meant that the person was sick. You see, we only had one bathroom in our home, and it was downstairs. We learned at an early age that if you were sick, you better sleep on the floor of the living room or on the couch. Mom hated nothing worse than cleaning up vomit on the stairway, mostly because that's where all of us parked our shoes at night, among other things. Only once do I remember our shoes receiving a new look of the unwanted prize of a half-digested meal. It was one of the few times my mother got upset. She always stressed to us to recognize that sick feeling and to take precautions. It made her mad when we didn't. I spent many a night on the couch when I was sick. With six kids in the family, it was rare not to see someone sleeping on the couch in the morning.

It was time to get this summer vacation under way. I walked down the hallway past my sister's room. I could hear her record player playing one of her new records. Dickie Lee was singing and telling the story about a girl named "Patches." I knew the artists because I always examined the 45's when she would buy a new one. The labels were all so different, and it got to the point where we didn't have to look at the information on the record to play the choice we wanted. We just recognized the label and threw it on to play. Claudia was the first to get her own record player. To me, it was the best thing ever, next to baseball cards and a bicycle, of course. Claudia, being my older sister, was and still is, very maternal. I always loved her for that. She was peeking out of the doorway, and she had her arm out waiting to reel me in. She was still in her pajamas, but she had her hair combed, and two braids lay on each side of her head. Her bangs were cut straight and made a perfect line above her eyebrows. Her face sported a few freckles accented with a huge smile. A few years earlier, I heard someone say that Claudia and Pippy Longstocking were twins that had been separated at birth. A few minutes later, my mom was explaining to me what a "figure of speech" was.

Even though the music was playing, it was hard to get by her room without her hearing me coming down the hallway. The old, squeaking floorboards were hard to miss. Claudia always had mystery and drama in her voice. Occasionally, she had a secret that she always made me promise not to tell. She snatched my arm and yanked me into her room before I knew it.

"Guess what," she said in a loud whisper.

"What?"

"I have a birthday list," she said as she held a piece of paper up in the air.

"Let me see what you have."

As I took the list, I noticed that it was torn out of a wire-bound notebook. Small straggles of paper were still holding on for dear life. She had five numbers written on the page. The number one item was written in big red capital letters. It said, *"JIMMY LOGAN."* I didn't even look at the rest of the list before asking her, "Who is Jimmy Logan?"

Without hesitation, she immediately said, "My new boyfriend, silly." I raised my eyebrows and said, "Oh."

"Pat," she said while touching my arm, "true love will never die you know." I nodded my head, not really understanding the seriousness of her statement. "Will you walk over to his house with me today?" she asked. I was trying to find an excuse in my head not to go when she quickly added, "I'll buy you a Coke downtown if you come with me."

How could I resist that? I agreed and later we took that walk a few blocks away, so she could see where her newest love lived. Records, gum, a diary, and a hula hoop rounded out the birthday list. Claudia was soon to be eleven. I was eight, and this summer was going to be a special one.

I came back into the present as my mom called from the kitchen, "Come on, Pat, we have to get going soon." I descended the stairs almost as fast as I climbed them the night before.

2

Mom was a magnificent cook, and I couldn't wait to eat. I walked past the stove where slabs of bacon were calling my name. I picked up a warm piece and snapped off a bite.

"Sit, sit," Mom said.

I was savoring every bite when I wondered if college food would ever match up to Mom's home cooking. I produced a small smile and knew better.

"Do you have all your money?" Mom asked.

I felt the pocket that held it and nodded. The last six months of work paid for my tuition and dorm room; any money left over would be for extra things. Mom plucked something from the top of the refrigerator and walked towards me. She held an envelope in her hand. The top flap was loose, and she pulled it back and sorted through some pictures that were filed in the small white encasement. Her face smiled when she found the one for which she was looking. She placed a picture of me in my little league uniform on the table. It was an old black and white photo taken right before my very first game. I remembered when it was taken, but I didn't recall ever seeing the actual photo.

"Man, it seems like yesterday when that was taken," I said. A rush of reality ran over me. How fast time flies…

During the summer months, my life revolved around baseball. The Milwaukee Braves were a few years away from being the Atlanta Braves. If someone had told me that the Braves were moving, I would have wrestled them to the ground. I loved the Braves, especially *Hammering* Hank Aaron. When the word came down that the Braves were indeed moving to Atlanta, I immediately jumped ship. I rooted for the team that was the closest, and more importantly, the team that I could watch every Sunday on TV, the Chicago Cubs. The only time I wanted the Cubs to lose was when the Braves played them which wouldn't happen for two years.

1963...is the year I started my baseball career. I was eight and my dad was my coach. Dad was one of the many founders of the little league program. He coached my two older brothers in their first years of the league, and now it was my turn. The baseball program itself consisted of two leagues. The little league had kids ranging from eight to ten year olds, and the big league consisted of kids ranging from eleven to thirteen. One thing I found out was that most eight-year olds didn't play much, even if their dad was the coach. I played my league regulated three innings and got my one, and if I got lucky, two times up to bat. I couldn't understand why I didn't play every inning. I felt I knew baseball as well as anybody, and my skills were as good as any ten-year old. After all, Chris, one of my older brothers, taught me everything that I needed to know about "America's Favorite Past Time." As the season progressed, I went through a routine before every game. It made me feel like I had enough playing time. Of course, the most important thing about playing organized baseball was the uniform.

"Can't you iron any faster than that, Mom?" I asked. My mom looked up and smiled.

"Why Hon, you know the game doesn't start until six."

"Yeah, I know, but geez, it's almost four," I quickly pled my case. Mom was slumped over the ironing board running the iron over my uniform. A can of spray starch was close at hand. She looked so capable with her sleeveless housedress on.

"Go get the rest of your uniform on. By that time I'll be done here," she suggested.

"But," I tried to say. She gave her head a nod toward the neatly folded pile in the distance.

"Go on," she said in an orderly fashion.

"Oh, okay," I said with my head down. I sat on the floor and pulled my white tube socks to the knee. One of the best parts of getting dressed was next. The ultimate feeling of putting on the stirrups was better than Saturday morning. I knew I was a baseball player when those were on. The stirrups were all red, with small white lines encircling the leg. Wow, they looked so professional. I just loved them. Standing in my underwear I called, "Ya done yet?" Mom walked over to me and handed me the top and bottom. The white pants were still warm from the iron.

"Here ya go, Hon," she said with a grin, "how you get these things so dirty I'll never know." I knew the answer to that. I couldn't get them on fast enough as I threw the pants on first. The elastic bottom below the knee made the uniform complete. *I just wish the top had a number on it....# 44, just like Hank Aaron...Hammering Hank,* I thought. The bleached white bottoms of my uniform had a small, deep red line running down the side. It made me look like a real **Milwaukee Brave.**

"Thanks Ma," I said, as I pulled my cap over my head.

She shouted back, "You're welcome, Pat. See ya at the game, Hon!"

I grabbed my glove and took off out the door, through the porch, and down the steps. I ran with a mission in mind. *I had to get there first!* The little league diamonds were right across the street in back of the elementary school. I was so glad that I finally was old enough to play. Eight years old sure seemed like an old age to wait to play ball; I played baseball since I could walk. Chris made sure I had all the skills. Fly balls, grounders, one-hoppers, bunting, and pitching were all part of the spring training Chris prepared for me. I knew I was ready. I was approaching the diamonds in a dead run. *This is so great! No one is here yet.* I ran to the bench and threw my glove; it hit the top and fell off. *I wouldn't need that now.* I looked quickly around to make sure I was all alone. A quick check affirmed it was safe. The lines on the diamond were all neatly done, and the field was completely dragged. It was almost too nice to step on, but I knew what had to be done. I peeled over to home plate and stood, facing the pitcher's mound.

"Okay Roger, pitch one in to me," I said to no one, looking toward the mound. Roger was the local ten-year old who just so happened to be the best pitcher in the league. I feared him. "Now batting for the Braves...playing right field... Pat...Daaaaavis...," my mind was applauding the announcement. I stepped into the batter's box, making sure I didn't mess up the lines. "Come on, Roger, put one down the pipe," I whispered to myself, as though someone might actually hear me. Roger wound up and whipped one in. I quickly dodged out of the way of the ball that could only be seen by me.

"Wow that was close!" I yelled. The pitcher had given me a little "chin music." I heard that expression listening to the game last night and liked it. I planted that expression in the back of my mind, wanting to ask my buddy Richey Clark if he had heard that one yet. Sometimes words are correct for an action. That was one of them. *Chin music huh, Roger? You chicken. Afraid I may knock one down your throat? Come on...Give me something I can hit!* My mind was sassing. He wound up again. And here's the pitch. SMASH...I swung my imaginary bat and saw the ball fly to the outfield. It was heading for the gap. I was hauling as fast as I could toward first base when I noticed the first base coach (having a striking resemblance to the Brave's manager) was wind-milling me for two. "Oh yeah, a double," I proudly said to myself as I ran like the wind, little legs just a churning. I'd have to hurry though.

I said out loud, "OH MY GOD...IT'S GOING TO BE CLOSE...HERE COMES DAVIS...HE'S SLIDING...," as I went feet first into second base (just like Chris showed me) "HE'S SAFE!" I yelled. I was standing on second and imitating the ump with both arms sticking out like an airplane. I quickly hopped on the base and looked around to make sure no one was here yet to observe my imaginary game. *Safe again,* I thought to myself. I could hear the phantom base coach at third, yelling to me, *Davis, we need you to score! All your speed baby! All your speed!* I gave him the nod, knowing I would score. The next sound I heard was the crack of the bat. I was thinking of one thing only: *The crowd will go completely wild when I score.* As I rounded third, the thought went into my head, *Be careful. Don't mess up those base lines.* I often wondered if I had the chance to score in a real game, if I would slide the same way. As I approached home, I made sure I came in from the front of the plate. I sure didn't want to scar the lines the "little league line man" made. I weaved toward the front of the plate while my mind raced. I slid only to hear the umpire call the obvious: **"SAFE!"** I stood raising my arms into the air, knowing I just scored the winning run. *"DAVIS DOES IT AGAIN WITH HIS SPEED....THE CROWD GOES WILD!"* If my mom could only see me, she'd know why my uniform needed to be washed after every game. I walked with triumph back to the bench to wait for my team. Only guessing which teammate would be the first to tell me, "Hey Davis, tell your ma to wash your uniform!" No matter, Mom would wash it, and I would be here two hours before my next game started. And again, I would give my mom a reason to wash my uniform.

3

As the dark blue station wagon (showing the wear of six kids) rolled north towards LaCrosse, I sat in the front seat alongside my youngest sister Mary. We had a nine passenger vehicle, and all three people were sitting in the front. We were close but familiarly comfortable. I looked out the window and saw the homes of our neighbors…

1965…Our neighborhood had three main families, each had four boys. There was also Oz. Oz deserves his own time, but not right now. We were all just a few years apart in age, and we all lived within walking distance. Tommy Weaver was one year younger than Eddie, and

Mike followed behind Tommy by a few years. I think we hung with the Weavers more than any other kids because of their lifestyle. They were a lot like us. We could throw a blanket over a clothesline, call it a tent, and sleep in it to prove it. We also took turns for sleepovers. Their dad passed away suddenly a few years earlier, and their mother was left with four boys in the house. I always enjoyed Mrs. Weaver. Even as a child, I understood she had her hands full. She seemed to handle life very well being a single mother and all. She always opened her door to the Davis boys, and my mother did the same for her kids.

The other family was the Haas family. They were more organized than a new book of matches. Their father worked at a local shop, and his job hours were like clockwork. Every day, Monday through Friday, he was home at noon for lunch and home for good at five. Mrs. Haas ran a tight ship. She was strict in our eyes because of how *our* lifestyle was. She actually made her children put their toys away, and the kids knew better than to leave their coats on the floor. Their home was always neat, and they had a garden that probably could have won awards.

Mr. Haas spent many an hour in that garden. Peter and Jake Haas were two other neighbors with whom Eddie and I played. I think they enjoyed playing with us and the Weavers because they could let their hair down a bit. When things got a little crazy and askew, they usually retreated home. Peter and Jake had two older brothers, Matt and Brian. Brian was Chris's age, and Matt was two years older than me. Matt always had a job. He had a paper route and also worked for Gil's Bike Shop. The bike shop was tucked deep into an alley. Its location was not ideal for advertisement, but it was great for kids traveling downtown. You had to pass it if you were heading to the lake or the campus where all of the city baseball and football games were played. There were other ways to get to these places, but the alley was simply a shortcut. Gil always had displays sitting outside. The first time I saw a stingray was at Gil's. It had a bright yellow frame with a black banana seat. The handlebars were high in the air, topped off with black handle grips with yellow stripes. It looked like tiger stripes. The tires were slicks. No tread, just wide, flat black tires with white lettering on them. God, it was beautiful! I bet I stared at that bike for half an hour taking in every detail. At thirty-five dollars, it was totally out of my league. It might as well have been a million dollars, because I wasn't going to ever have enough money to buy something like that. I could dream though, and that was free. Besides, I'd been saving my allowance for six months for a brand-new Wilson baseball glove autographed by Luis Aparicio. I saw it in the Sears and Roebuck catalog, and it was only twenty dollars. With a glove, you didn't have to worry about it breaking down, just breaking it in.

Matt was the first on our block with a ten speed. It had all the devices a bicycle could possibly have: a speedometer, a horn, and most importantly, head and taillights. When it got dark out, you weren't supposed to ride your bike unless you had a light. The local police made it their mission to let you know the laws. Having gears on a bike was a whole new concept to most kids. The fact that you had to shift gears made the driver look like a genius. But the one major drawback any ten-speed bike had was the fact that you couldn't lay rubber on the sidewalk when you came to a skidding stop. That was one feature most kids couldn't live without. Once Matt placed his new Schwinn on blocks and took us through the gears as he peddled in place. We all thought that was so cool. I tried to convince my brother Chris to come over for a quick demo, and he just laughed at the idea. Chris was probably thinking how simple I was. I just shrugged my shoulders and ran back over to see it again. Matt could afford this bike because of his many jobs. The rest of the neighborhood was too busy playing all summer. Matt was always building something. He was slightly built, and I don't think I ever saw him without glasses. He was the first kid I ever saw that had a pencil with a clip that conveniently fastened to his front pocket. He was constantly designing and drawing on anything close, to help his calculations. He was usually building model cars, but when the Fourth of July approached, he worked on the ultimate bomb. Recently, it was a go cart that consumed his time. The fact that his dad had a great workshop made building things easier. All the Haas boys were more than capable of using the shop, of course, with the criteria that it was cleaned up when they were done. Many times we would be in the Haas's basement playing, and Mr. Haas would come home at five, walk into his shop, and mention to one of the boys that something was not in place. They would hop up and take care of their father's request immediately. I admired that. At our house, it was nearly impossible to find a tool. We used a butter knife for a screwdriver, and a steak knife came in handy when we needed a Phillips. The closest we could come to a flashlight was a candle. My dad claimed he had tools once, but my older brothers lost so many of them he stopped buying them. I had no way of knowing if that was true; all I knew was that we had no tools. Once, I stumbled across a pair of pliers in the backyard that looked like it had been there before time, so I guess maybe his story held some merit.

Matt spent many hours building his go cart. He had been working on it all summer, and we all were waiting in anticipation for him to finish. Everyday we played baseball in the field, and as we walked home, there was Matt toiling away. He always gave us his updates and when he thought he was going to be done. "August" was his most consistent answer. The day finally arrived. He rolled the metal-framed beast out onto the driveway. It was pretty much bar stock with a motor on the back. Eddie and I, along with the rest of the neighbors, stood in awe as we examined his creation.

“Does the motor run?” I asked.

I think Matt was waiting for that question all day because without hesitation he walked over to the motor, wrapped the rope around the flywheel, and gave it a tug. Nothing happened. He did it again and still nothing happened. A little snicker came from somewhere in our group, and Matt quickly put an end to any doubt when he choked the motor and tugged harder this time. It gave a sound of life and quit. He pushed the choke back in, wrapped the rope, and confidently said, “It'll go this time.” He was right. It coughed a bit and fired up. We all anticipated the thrill of driving it. We all wanted first dibs. The way things like this were decided was simple. The first person to say “FIRST!” was first, discussion over. I marveled over the black 7.5 HP Briggs and Stratton motor, vibrating even faster as Matt revved it up. Black smoke bellowed out of the very familiar lawn mower-like muffler. We were all screaming and chattering like school girls with the anticipation of driving the steel apparatus.

Matt shut the engine down, and unfortunately for Eddie, his voice was heard saying, "FIRST!"

Fifteen minutes later, I was holding Eddie's badly damaged arm. The throttle had stuck, and in an attempt of trying to turn the go cart around, he flipped out of the metal contraption and virtually tore the back part of his arm off. We were five minutes away from home, but it seemed like it took an hour to get there. I was crying my head off, holding my hands around Eddie's gaping wound. Even with a choke hold on his arm, my hands weren't big enough to entirely cover his shredded triceps. For some odd reason, I didn't want the blood to hit the ground as it streamed down the angle of my arms and dripped off the point of my elbows. I tried to coordinate my stride so the blood would hit my pants and shoes as though I was trying to save it for future use. Your mind does funny things when thrown into a crisis. We just wanted to get home to show our mom what terrible news we had for her. My mother was resting on the couch as we entered the living room.

I just screamed, "EDDIE'S HURT!" Tears and snot were running from my face as I handed Eddie off to Mom.

She grabbed his arm and screamed, "Jesus Christ what happened?"

I blubbered something about a go cart. I wasn't making much sense because the sounds that were coming from my mouth didn't sound at all like words. She didn't have time to interpret what I was saying. Mom quickly grabbed a towel from the laundry room and wrapped it around his arm right below the shoulder. He was bleeding so badly the blood was evident on the outside of the towel as she rushed to the car. I stood in blood crying and asking if he was going to die. She kept telling me, "NO!"

I'll bet I asked her twenty times as she tended to Eddie. "Is he going to die? Is he going to be okay? Are they going to have to cut off his arm?" She stopped answering me after a while. She had to concentrate on what she was doing. She didn't have time to console me.

She said, "Stay here, he'll be alright," as she rushed him off to the medical center. I waited at home, crying in the bathtub, trying to scrub off the smell of blood and the thought of Eddie dying. Eddie did come home, and he was fine, but not before receiving multiple stitches in his muscle along with over a dozen more on the outside of his arm. I was so relieved to see him. He was the first kid to receive stitches, but he wouldn't be the last. I followed up a few weeks later, cutting off the underside of my index finger throwing a busted bottle top at an alley wall. I only got six stitches. A few years later, another go cart accident severed my Achilles tendon. That was the last time either one of us drove a go cart. We didn't hang around Matt too much after that incident. Anyway, we had his brothers to play with, along with the Weavers.

4

We were heading west toward Madison, and the frost on the window of our car couldn't hide the sight of barren fruit trees. The protective fence that surrounded them made me think of a time when picking apples was an intricate part of summer. It was only fun when we were in an orchard that was off limits…

1964…If we weren't playing ball in the field, we were climbing some apple tree eating everything in sight as we advanced up. It was common practice to tuck in your shirt, toss apples down through the collar, and walk away with enough to fill our bellies for the next half hour or so, I'm not sure about the rest of the neighborhood, but eating in between meals around our house didn't go over very well. If my mom saw us eating other than when it was meal time, she thought we didn't get enough to eat when we *did* eat. Her theory was to make enough for an army and allow us to go back for as much as we wanted, never walking away hungry. Maybe that's my theory, but with six kids in the family, and four of them being boys, I doubt if she had any other choice than to make enough for an army. So, if we could snatch a few apples here and there, our constant hunger wouldn't be an issue.

We, as well as our neighbors, all had apple trees, but the ones we weren't supposed to pick always tasted better. For instance, Old Man Hardy had an orchard that had a fence around it. The fact that it was fenced in meant one thing, those apples had to be special. Once word got around that the taste of those apples were the best in Wisconsin, the invasion began. We managed to dig a small hole around the base of the fence, and at dusk, we would crawl under to fill our shirts. Rumors were that you didn't want to get caught by Old Man Hardy. One story circulated that he was so mean he would beat you with a stick until you passed out, and then he would throw you back over the fence. His voice alone would make you shiver in August. A few times we thought we were all alone as we crawled under the fence, and we heard him from a distance yell, "GET OUT OF MY ORCHARD!" It's amazing how much faster you can go under a fence when you're scared. He lived right next door to the Weavers, and they rarely stole apples from him, probably because his presence was too fresh for them to mess with him. It didn't stop us or Peter and Jake Haas. We looked at it as a challenge. Peter put all the ugly rumors aside when he was the first to get caught by Old Man Hardy.

The entire length of the fence was concealed with bushes, so you couldn't see the orchard. For years, we didn't even know that there were apples over there. Perhaps the bushes were planted there for that reason, who knows. Peter went first, as I waited my turn to crawl under the fence. He was on his belly using his hands to throw the fresh dirt aside that covered the hole we made the year before. As Peter dug, he reminded me of our Beagle, Henry, digging for a jelly bean we had thrown in the grass. He finally removed enough soil to make his way under. The back pockets of his jeans along with the heels of his Red Ball Jets were the only things exposed. As I looked at his tennis shoes, a thought came to me. It seemed like only yesterday when I had to decide which shoes I wanted. I had to weigh out the difference between Red Ball Jets and PF Flyers. The choice of shoe brand really wasn't that difficult; I figured in a few months my shoes would be shot, and if I made a bad choice now, I could go with the other brand next time. Both shoes were black, high tops. The Red Ball Jets had the red ball placed directly over the side ankle bone. The contrast of the small, rubber red ball on the black made them very cool. The PF Flyers advertisement was enough for me: *"THEY MAKE YOU RUN FASTER AND JUMP HIGHER!"* Heck, I went with the performance qualities rather than the look. You just never knew when you would have to run faster and jump higher.

I was hoping this situation wouldn't have to prove the ad correct. When I saw Peter's rear end and legs suddenly move with more speed than normal, I knew he was being pulled by someone or something from the other side. He looked like a string being sucked into a vacuum cleaner. The obvious voice on the other side proved it was no vacuum, but the worse case scenario. I could just imagine Old Man Hardy grinning from ear to ear as he nabbed his culprit. He was old, but he wasn't stupid. Out of forty trees, one was nearly picked clean. It didn't take him long to figure out where we were coming in to steal apples. I'm sure he planned his whole evening for this little surprise. If he would have been real smart, he would have waited for both of us to get on the other side of the fence. No such luck. When I heard Peter let out a yell, the jump higher part of the shoes proved true and the run faster came soon after. I didn't see Peter the rest of the evening or most of the next day. I kept a watchful eye on his house and assumed the worst.

When we got the *Watertown Daily Times* newspaper the next day, I was hoping *not* to see Peter's picture in the paper with the headline: "Boy Missing." I waited until after I went through the whole paper before going over to Peter's house to see if he was in one piece. As it turned out, he was fine; he had only gotten bawled out by his folks. At least he was alive to tell us that his ordeal wasn't as bad as we all imagined. A week later, I discovered Old Man Hardy had a regular job other than waiting for trespassing kids on the other side of his fence. I realized the thrill was gone and the challenge was over when I found myself eating an apple in the middle of his orchard in broad daylight while he was at work. It was no longer the forbidden fruit.

5

It didn't take me long to realize Mom was taking a route other than the one that was so carefully planned. "Mom," I said, "why are we taking Highway 14 instead of the interstate? I-90 is so much faster."

"Sometimes the fastest way isn't always the best," she explained, "besides this way we can see more of the countryside." I couldn't blame her for wanting to see more. Our travels usually consisted of going to the south side of Chicago to see our relatives. My anxiety was building up as we got closer to our destination. "A bakery in LaCrosse bought Dad's freezers," Mom said.

"Yes, I remember Dad saying something about that."

...From the time I turned thirteen, every Monday through Saturday, I worked at our family's bakery. Dad would call home at 5 A.M. No one else would answer the phone at that time in the morning but me, since I was the one for which the call was intended. There was never a conversation, just a simple, "Ya up?"

And a quick answer of, "Yep."

The sound of the telephone meant it was time to go to work and to fry doughnuts. My dad owned the bakery since 1953. Initially, he took the bakery job to help Uncle Rudy. It was shortly thereafter that Uncle Rudy had a fatal heart attack, and my dad bought the business from Aunt Jean. As we grew up, all of us kids had duties to fulfill in the bakery. Since I was out for sports, I had to work in the morning. My time after school was limited to practice and homework. Okay, mostly practice, but my work was minimal compared to my dad's schedule.

Dad would get up at nine in the evening to go to the bakery, and he would return home the next morning at nine, twelve hours of work, six days a week. In the bakery's prime, Dad made bread for all three schools, pies for the new Conoco Oasis Truck Stop, cherry tarts for the Gobbler motel, and hundreds of hamburger buns on Friday for the Legion. The world-famous Legion "Slider," in my opinion, was, and still is, the best hamburger made in the area. The fact that it's fried in a vat of grease created the name. It was common to stop in the bakery after school on Friday to help Mom slice the many pans of buns. Even with an automatic slicer, it was time consuming. The life of a Baker is not an ordinary life, and after twenty years of that labor, my dad pulled the plug on the bakery business. Dad's contention was that the high price of sugar was making it tough for him to make a marginal profit. I believe that the creation of the bakery in the grocery stores killed the independent bakery business. Either way, I really couldn't blame him for not wanting to work seventy-two hours a week anymore. All those hours of working alone would make anybody go nuts or drink. My dad chose the later.

Our family worked through his alcoholism, and Mom carried most of the burden so her children wouldn't have to. Eleven years after leaving the bakery, Dad finally got help and attended his first AA meeting. Dad's problems never overshadowed the perks of having a bakery. We never realized how lucky we were having fresh bakery goods until we were forced to eat store bought bread. I had a hard time believing people actually ate bread like that. Having fresh bakery goods everyday was something we took for granted, as did our poor miniature beagle, Henry (short for Henrietta), who was not so miniature. A twenty-pound ham on four feet would have been the best description for her.

Henry was the recipient of anything we didn't want to eat. I would come home in the morning from work holding a white bakery bag, and she would waddle into the kitchen like a small bear lumbering into a camp looking for a handout. She would sit on the kitchen floor and routinely go through her tricks until we tossed down a torn-off piece of a jelly-filled doughnut. Her tricks were always in the same order. First, she'd put up her paw. That never worked, but it took the least amount of effort. The next trick she did was to try to sneeze. It took us a while to teach her that one. Henry would shake her head without the sound several times until she finally put a grand effort into blowing air out of her snout like it was filled with pepper. We always rewarded her at that point because we really didn't want her to go to her next trick. It was the trick she knew the best, but she had the hardest time doing it. Rolling over was a trick alright. She resembled a small barrel of beer lying on her side that was only filled a quarter of the way. She would make the attempt of trying to roll over, and as she got to the peak of her roll, she would roll back the same way she came. She had to actually get momentum to complete the stunt. It usually took at least three attempts, but she got much praise by anyone that actually saw the event.

Eddie's role at the bakery was to wash all the pots and pans after school. The double-basin, stainless steel sink that held the pans was huge but not big enough to hold the entire lot of work. I had my job done in the morning, and I rarely had to do Eddie's work. Occasionally, he had his friends help him. They usually did it for several handfuls of chocolate chips or leftover bakery goods. It was a win-win deal for Eddie. What friend wouldn't want to help him for free doughnuts, or anything else that was lying around. But having friends help in the bakery usually created mischief, especially when Deke Ruebens, Dad's good friend and owner of the café right next door, was around. Deke was short in stature but had some thickness to him. He was always wearing white, white pants, white tee shirt, topped off with a white paper chef's hat. He had jet-black hair with a patch of white that was only seen when his hat was removed. He loved a practical joke; so naturally, he could appreciate one being pulled on him occasionally. At first, I think Deke thought he could do all the joking around he wanted and no one would retaliate. He found out just the contrary.

There was an alley between the back of the bakery and the café that he would have to walk through to get to the back door of the café. Occasionally, when Deke saw Eddie working after school, his practical-joking imagination would go into motion. Once, he piled a bunch of garbage in front of the bakery door so Eddie had a hard time getting the door open. At first, Eddie had no idea that Deke was doing this until my dad smiled and told us what the *Real Deke* was like. We didn't know it at the time but the best part about pulling one on Deke was the colorful language that followed. As an adolescent, hearing an adult cuss with true conviction was quite honestly hilarious. That alone fed our need to keep antagonizing him. We thought we were pretty clever by laying our bicycles in front of the backdoor of the café. That way he'd have to step around them or move them to get inside. We watched through the side windows of the bakery, snickering as Deke approached. It didn't take us long to realize he wasn't about to step around anything. He picked up the bikes and heaved them in the pile of weekly café garbage that was at the end of the alley. After tip toeing through the old food and empty cans to retrieve our bikes, we knew we had to give this more thought. We made the mistake of thinking Deke forgot about what we had done. The next day we would get a handful of grease as we tried to open the door to the bakery. We knew where that came from. So, war was proclaimed without an official document.

The bakery's flat roof provided a great place to develop our next attack. Even though the weather forecast called for mostly sunny with a very slight chance of showers, a bushel basket of water balloons would rain on Deke the next day. I don't know what was funnier, watching Deke get pelted or listening to his swearing. We laughed until our sides ached. We knew we won the battle, but not the war. Nothing would happen for nearly a week or just long enough for us to let our guard down. He was pretty smart, for an adult. His revenge was easy because he had a key to the back door of the bakery. One morning, I came to work and tripped over a bunch of empty cans that lay right inside the door. I looked up from the floor and asked my dad why he left them there.

He looked down at me and said, "Hey, you and Eddie started something with Deke, I'm not about to get in the way of that."

When I came home from work that morning, I told Eddie what happened. It gave him all day to think of something. I had practice that afternoon, so Eddie was going to have to take care of it on his own. He needed help with his next trick, so he had one of his buddies look out for him as he washed the pans. In the storage room of the bakery, there were piles of ingredients such as: fifty-pound bags of flour, sugar, powdered sugar, coconut, chocolate chips, pecans, and various other goods. We had so many bags that they were stacked on top of each other. It created a perfect lookout since the windows in the room were rather high. The windows faced the parking lot where Deke would park. Eddie's friend, Johnny, lay on the bags waiting for Deke. Eddie knew he would be coming to work sooner or later.

Just about the time Eddie was finishing and giving up hope, Deke pulled into his parking spot. Johnny yelled from the lookout tower. Eddie quickly got into position next to the wall fan that faced the alley. The two foot square industrial wall fan was our only source of relief from the summer humidity. You could not have an air conditioned bakery. Air conditioning would slow up the process of yeast to rise. This fan was powerful enough to turn a Kleenex tissue into confetti. It only had one speed: Jet engine. The sound it gave off was powerful, and yet the low hum was deceiving. The three huge fan blades were encased in a protective cage to prevent anyone from turning their hands into hamburger. While Deke got out of his car, Eddie turned on the fan. The roar of the motor gave off the familiar sound. From the alley, the protective flaps opened the eyes of a sleeping giant. Eddie waited until the perfect moment. Deke walked head level to the fan, and Eddie tossed a cup of flour toward the blades. It sucked it out so fast it didn't make a sound. Deke didn't know what hit him. His hat flew off, and his ear was solid white. One side of his face looked like a mime and the other was flesh tone. To make matters worse, Johnny and Eddie laughed out loud, so Deke knew who did it.

"SON OF A," rang out. The more he swore, the more they laughed. They turned the fan off immediately after the deed, so the sound of the fan wouldn't drown out any of the language. Johnny had a laugh that was almost antagonizing. He stood by the screen door and heckled him. Deke turned and tried to open the door, but Johnny latched the door seconds before he pulled the handle. When he couldn't get the door open, Johnny laughed even harder. Eddie flicked the fan on again, hopi temper would let his guard down. He had to pass the fan again after trying the door. Sure enough, he walked right in front of it, and Eddie gave him a second dose. This time, for some odd reason, Deke looked directly into the fan, as though he was still trying to figure out what had happened the first time. "GOD DAMMIT!" he screamed. What a perfect ending to a war. He had had enough. Later that evening, he told my dad of the incident, and Dad told us he laughed the entire time. In a way, Eddie was relieved, because of the way Deke carried on. He didn't want Deke to have hard feelings. Apparently, he didn't. It was probably the first time anyone ever got the best of him, and he could appreciate that.

Working in the morning was my exclusive time with Dad. We talked about many things, mostly sports topics. Whenever he gave me advice, he always used the same line, "You might not agree with this, and I know you'll do it your own way, but..." He was right; I usually did do it my own way and found out that most of the time he was right in his advice. But I figured, what did he know?

He'd been an adult his whole life. What did he know about kids' problems?

On the other end of the scale, there was Ernie "Grandpa" Snyder. He was Dad's helper on Saturdays. He wasn't really our Grandpa, but we were taught to call him that. Ernie's dad was a baker in Milwaukee, so he knew the trade. Dad always paid him with bakery goods. He lived right outside of Lake Mills on a farm, and we would visit him occasionally to hunt and camp on his property. His round face donned big black-rimmed glasses, and his hair was as white as snow. His dentured smile ran from ear to ear, and he walked with a pronounced limp, caused from having his leg busted in several spots as a kid. Apparently, he was hit by a car at a young age. That's what he told me anyway. You just never knew what to believe when Ernie told you something. Half the time you didn't know if he was kidding you or telling you the truth. Both ways were told to you in the same manner. He would always get the raised eyebrow from my dad when I would ask for advice. I was directing the question to Dad, but Ernie would always chime in and give me the answer I wanted, and not the one that was proper. He called me Champ ever since I won my first conference wrestling title. This was a typical line from Ernie: "Champ, love 'em all, drink 'til you're sick, and smoke a cigar cause they're good for ya." You can see why Dad had to keep him in check. I knew he was saying those things to get a rise out of me, and I knew better, but his voice returned in my head, as occasionally I had too many drinks.

Saturday mornings were always an adventure, and more times than not Ernie and Dad were on their way to a snoot full by the time I got there. Coincidentally, Saturday was the only time things got burned in the oven. I was usually at fault though, according to Ernie, especially when it came to the Pecan Crispies; also know as "Elephant Ears." I was off doing my usual duties of frying doughnuts when an all too familiar groan came from the adult end of the workbench. After many times, I knew that sound was proceeded by swearing and throwing the blame at me for burning the Crispies that were put in the oven thirty minutes earlier and should have been taken out fifteen minutes sooner. When I got blamed the first time, I argued my point that the oven was not my responsibility, but I found out in time that the only time I was responsible was when things got burned. I took the blame in stride and humor. Once, Dad and Ernie were up front in the store of the bakery, and I took the Crispies out in time and threw a towel over them as they cooled. Thirty minutes later, I asked them if the Crispies were done, and they both panicked as they ran towards the oven. They opened the oven to discover that they had miraculously disappeared. When Ernie saw them on the rack, he could only say with a smile, "It's about time you did your job!"

The brandy usually brought out more fatherly advice than what I was used to, whether I wanted it or not, and Ernie was full of suggestions as well. Once, as a senior in high school, the subject of women came up, and both my dad and Ernie were feeling no pain. My dad had enough dignity so he kept his thoughts to himself, but Ernie had nothing to lose, so he cut loose. Of course, being a senior, when he started to talk about making love to a lady, although I was inexperienced, the language he was using was not foreign. The liquor was in charge, and his lips were saying things that had my dad looking at him very curiously. He was wondering where and how far he was going to go with this conversation or in this case, his lecture. He was soon describing how a woman liked to be kissed and where. At this point, I was laughing and Dad was clearing his throat. Ernie continued while grabbing an apron and tying it onto my dad's hips. Dad already had an apron on as he faced the bench rolling out dinner rolls. Ernie tied the long part of the apron toward the backside of my dad. Dad just shrugged his shoulders and continued to work as Ernie went on. When he flung the apron up, grabbed Dad's shoulders, and started gyrating his hips toward Dad, Dad turned around and stopped him. "Get to work, old man; I'm not paying you to act like a fool!" Ernie just howled with laughter as he staggered around trying to get his wits. Dad was saying something under his breath as I laughed right along with Ernie.

Five years of working in the bakery gave me more that just an education and a good work ethic. It gave me a different idea of the word "work." Before working there, I thought the word meant something unpleasant. I found out it was enjoyable, especially when you had fun doing it. Dad and Ernie made sure of that.

6

Driving on Highway 14 was altogether different than taking the interstate. In the first place, it seemed like it was taking forever to go one hundred and sixty miles. The way I figured it, by the time we got to LaCrosse, the semester would be over, and we could turn around and go back, just in time for spring. We were an hour into the trip, and we had gone approximately forty miles. I was beginning to think Mom was taking her time on purpose. I was constantly wrenching my neck to peek at the speedometer. After the third time, my mom asked, "What are you looking at, Hon?"

"I just wanted to see how fast we were going, that's all," I said, feeling a bit guilty about getting caught.

Mom looked at the dash and said, "Looks like we are going just fast enough."

"What, fifty?"

Mary leaned over to take a quick look at the speedometer and said, "Yup."

"Hmm, when do you think we'll get there?" I asked.

Mom stared at the dash again looking closely with a slight squint in her eyes and said, "Around noon."

I thought to myself, *Noon which day?*

It was no use; all I could do was try to enjoy the ride. We slowed up as we approached the next town. A four way stop was in the center of the downtown we entered. There was a Chevy dealership to our left and a gas station to our right. Mom took a right and pulled in for gas. I thought, *This is just what we need, another break to make this trip longer.*

After the service station man threw the gas-hose nozzle in our car, he immediately started cleaning our windows. He had a rag in his back pocket that he pulled out to get any remaining marks off the glass as he finished.

"Check your oil?" he asked.

"Yes, please," Mom said, as if she was just waiting for him to ask.

I gave a huff. "Why don't we have him wash the car right away," I said under my breath.

"What?" Mom asked.

"Nothing," I said, looking straight ahead.

The oil checked out fine and Mom paid the man. She tried to pull away from the pump, but she had to wait for two small children standing in front of the car. One was a boy and the other a girl, who were dressed in many layers of winter clothing. They were probably no older than six. They had just walked out of the gas station, and I could see that they had a pack of Lifesavers. They were both trying to open it with their mittens on. It was so ridiculous, it was funny. We sat and watched them struggle as they tore tiny pieces of paper from the small cylinder. The little boy had his tongue out to help the effort along. After a few seconds went by with little progress, I felt like rolling down the window to yell instructions. My mom and sister thought it was perfect entertainment as they called the play by play that was going on in front of our car. Finally, they had the paper torn off, and they tried to break off a Lifesaver. I could tell by their faces that the Lifesavers were all stuck together in one large roll. The boy solved that problem. He bit off the top piece of candy and handed it to the girl. Without hesitation, she put it in her mouth. The boy then placed the pack in front of his mouth and snapped off a piece for himself with his front teeth. I tried to reach over to beep the horn to move them along, but my mom snatched my hand.

"They'll move," she said with a small smile and a gleam in her eyes. The kids looked like they didn't have a worry in the world. They certainly didn't have to think about serious things, like college. They walked away holding hands...

1961...I was holding her hand because I knew that was what I was supposed to do. Our hands were swaying back and forth with every step. My hand was sweating, but I didn't want to let go. I was small for the age of six, but she was just my size and a perfect match. I felt good but nervous. Katy had dark brown hair cut to curl nicely around her chin. Her face had a soft, smooth look to it. Her deep blue eyes were piercing, and she looked like a movie star. We approached the Methodist Church, and I knew we were halfway there. I had asked my mom that morning if I could walk Katy home after school. She must have known where she lived because she said it was alright. In a way, I was hoping she would have said no. I liked Katy, but I wasn't sure if I liked her well enough to receive a kiss for walking her home. I was beginning to wonder why I agreed to such a deal anyway.

It all started with the note I received from her after school. She handed it to me in the hallway as I was putting my jacket on. As I slid my hand through the sleeve, it was met by a folded piece of white notebook paper. I had no clue what it contained, and I would have never guessed that it would be an intricate part of walking her home. The note held a question that got me involved in this adventure. She instructed me NOT to open it until I got to my house. As I walked through the field on my way home, I held the note tightly in my hand and had the urge to look at it. I kept my promise and opened it while I stood in my bedroom. The note was printed in pencil, and I could see that her handwriting was very good. All of her letters were drawn just like we were taught by our teacher. I found myself looking at the beauty of her printing rather than actually reading the content of her note. The question she had written was simple: *DO YOU LIKE ME? CIRCLE ONE: YES OR NO.* I searched for a pencil in my desk drawer, found one, and neatly circled *YES*. I wanted the circle to be as neat as her printing so when I gave it back to her she could see my handwriting was just as good as hers, even if it was just a circle. My answer was simple enough, but by circling *YES*, it led to a second question from Katy; this time it wasn't written down.

The next day as I stood in the hallway hanging up my jacket, I saw Katy advancing towards me as she weaved through the students. She walked up to me, and we stood face to face. She was close enough that the tips of her shoes touched mine. Katy had one hand on her hip and the other hand was palm up.

A few days earlier I saw Claudia standing in the same position. Eddie and I decided it would be funny to swap heads on Claudia's Barbie and Ken dolls. Since Claudia always had her dolls naked while lying in their small, folding doll case, we thought that it would be a real shock for her when she opened the case and saw that Ken had boobs. We couldn't take full credit for the idea; our oldest brother Bob planted that seed in our heads hoping we would make it grow. Whenever Bob would tease Claudia to tears, Mom would give him a warning, and he'd leave her alone for a few days. But that didn't stop him from carrying out his plans by using his younger and vulnerable brothers. We had Ken's head firmly placed on Barbie's body when Claudia entered her bedroom. I still had Barbie's head in my hand, and all I could do was put my hand behind my back. When Claudia looked down and saw Ken, she let out a small gasp. Then she saw the headless body of the other doll in Eddie's hand. Before Claudia could say a word, Eddie handed the torso over to her. Claudia then focused her attention on me. She placed one hand on her hip and stuck out her other hand. I handed over the head expecting her to be mad. She wasn't mad at all; in fact, she completed the deed, and we all had a good laugh.

I handed Katy the note, and she opened it before taking off her jacket. I could see her eyes scanning my response. I thought she was marveling at my compass like circle, but she had more important things to ponder. She quickly asked me if I wanted to walk her home. It was only *after* I said yes that she told me she would kiss me when we got to her house. She gave me the impression that walking her home was the real reason to kiss me, but I think the perfect circle around the YES is what really impressed her and earned a kiss.

As we passed the church, she said, "I'm glad you're Catholic; that means we can get married." Well, that certainly made sense. I had a very brief vision of us standing at the altar exchanging vows. As we approached her house, my heart was pounding like a hammer. I knew she was going to kiss me because that was the agreement. Before I could give it anymore thought, she grabbed my coat, tugged it in her direction, and kissed me flat on the lips. It was over before I even had time to think. I was looking straight into her eyes with a dreamy look. She said, "Thank you for walking me home."

"I do," I said.

"Huh?" she said with a smile.

"I mean you're welcome," I said, as my head cleared. "See you tomorrow." I started for home, and the closer I got, the more energy I had. By the time I was a block away, I was running as hard as I could. I flew in the door and saw my mom sitting at the table in the dining room.

"What's wrong, Hon?" she asked.

I just smiled and said, "Nothing is wrong. Everything is alright." I wasn't sure if I was relieved that my ordeal was over or happy that it was just beginning.

7

I couldn't shake the vision of Katy and me standing in church. The many hours of my life I spent in church were truly amazing. I didn't miss a Sunday from the time I was conscious enough to know where I was going. Being Catholic meant that becoming an altar boy was a given, and with enough prayers from my mother, perhaps being ordained priest. I actually visited a seminary, but the deal breaker was the fact that they didn't have a wrestling program. If I wasn't committed enough to give up a sport, it probably was a good idea to scratch that career off my list. When I was eight, I was indoctrinated in the many lessons of being an altar boy. Some were taught by Father Patterson and some by older boys.

Father Patterson was a modern, free-spirited priest that welcomed the changes the Catholic Church had just authorized. One key change was making the whole service in English rather than in Latin. I also welcomed that change because mumbling my lines would sooner or later catch up to me. That was a lesson I learned from one of the older altar boys. Dave had many years under his belt, so he let me in on that little secret. He told me that no one hears what you're saying anyway, so don't waste your time learning Latin. He didn't have to twist my arm to stop me from studying a language and words I didn't understand. English was hard enough in school. Who needed a foreign language to mess with your mind? I certainly didn't. Eddie joined me my second year and by that time the whole service was in English. We were partners all the way through high school. I actually liked the duty; it made church go faster. Father Patterson was fun to be around, had a good sense of humor, and loved kidding with us. He was a tall man with dark brown-black hair. He had a flat top haircut, just like the teenagers wore. He wanted everyone to know he was "with it." He introduced modern songs and the first guitar mass to our congregation. With rock and roll making the scene, his new ways made our church grow. Many teenagers started to show up that I didn't even know belonged to our church. We even had a few teenage converts. The word spread that our mass was "The happening thing." As the years went by, Eddie and I went through our duties as good altar boys did. One year, at the conclusion of midnight mass, we were let in on some breaking news by some of the older boys. They told us about the wine in the cellar of the church basement. They assured us it was fine to take a little taste before each service, that it really was an acceptable thing to do. Eddie and I figured they were right. Who were we to argue with a few seventeen and eighteen year olds that had all this altar boy knowledge? Of course, they had to throw in a little comment that shook their credibility a bit, "Just don't get caught!"

The following Sunday, we were scheduled for the eleven o'clock mass. Eddie and I figured there was no time like the present to get our "little taste" in. The nine o'clock mass came before our service, so we had that going for us. Since Eddie and I slept in the same bedroom, we had all night to scheme a plan. The well-thought out, intricate plot was debated repeatedly and put together in less than five minutes.

Our Plan: We would get to the church around 9:30 while everyone was upstairs praying and singing. Then we would easily slip downstairs from the outside entrance to get our much accepted taste of wine. When it was 10:30, we would simply take the stairs up to the tabernacle, get dressed in our cassocks, and wait for Father Patterson to arrive. We would do the service, bid farewell to Father Patterson, and live happily ever after.

Reality: Eddie and I were in the basement by 9:30 on the dot, as planned. We could hear the congregation singing "Faith of Our Fathers" as we looked for the refrigerator. I was thinking to myself, *This is almost too easy.* Eddie found the old white Coldspot refrigerator. It was sitting all by itself away from the tables that were laid out for banquets, weddings, and funerals. I trotted over and opened the door to see two huge bottles filled to the brim. The liquid was light yellow, and I knew it had to be wine by the small glass, cone-shaped plug that was inserted into the top. *They had to be gallon jugs,* I thought, as I pulled one from its cool confines and carried it to the table. Eddie scrounged around for something to pour it in. He brought over a couple of coffee cups he had found in the cupboard and placed them side by side on the table. I hoisted the big bottle and poured each of us a full cup. I set the bottle down and put the glass plug back into the top as though we weren't going to drink anymore after "the acceptable taste."

Eddie looked at me and used a line we heard many times watching the western *Gunsmoke* on Saturday night, "Down the hatch." We both lifted our cups and took a cautionary sip. We knew immediately it was wine. Although we never drank it, we could tell by the smell of it. We certainly poured enough of it in Father Patterson's chalice to know what it was. After our initial taste, we drank the rest of it with ease.

"Another?" I asked Eddie, as I picked up the bottle.

"Why not," he quickly replied with a wink as he raised his glass as though he was calling the bartender over for another round.

We had the second drink down before you could say Mary Magdalene. The clock said 9:47, and we could hear the people exiting the church. If there was one thing you could count on, it was the amount of time a standard Catholic service took. Forty-five to fifty minutes was the range. No more, no less. To this day, I am still convinced that Vince Lombardi called the Pope and requested a forty-five minute mass so the Packer fans could get home in time for the game.

The wine was starting to take effect on us, and we decided to have "one for the road." Another phrase that was perfect for the occasion, I filled the cups one last time and carried the half empty jug towards the refrigerator. Eddie made the suggestion that we fill it with water so Father Patterson wouldn't find out. Even with a fuzzy head, it made sense. I held the jug under the faucet and filled it to the top. I pushed the glass plug in the top of the jug, and Eddie held the door of the refrigerator open as I placed the wine on the top shelf, just as it sat a few minutes earlier. Eddie and I sat back down next to our cups. We drank like two old cronies sitting at the Longbranch Saloon in Dodge City. At this point, if Doc Adams and Miss Kitty would have walked through the door, I would have called them over for a drink. With one leg going numb, I was beginning to feel a little bit like Chester.

The eleven 'o clock mass was the furthest thing from our minds. Before we knew it, the clock said 10: 36. Eddie looked tired. "We better get upstairs for church," I said.

"Sure, okay," Eddie said.

We weaved our way up the stairs and had our cassocks on before Father Patterson arrived. Everything was going as planned until Father informed me that I had my cassock on backwards. What did he expect; I had only worn it a few hundred times. The first clue should have been when I saw the buttons in the front. The Catholic Church was changing so much that I thought it was a new style or something. Father Patterson shook his head as he looked at me with some curiosity. Eleven o'clock soon came and mass began. The forty-five minutes went by quickly, and our well-executed plan was history. Only a few snafus had happened during the service that we didn't think were too major at the time. Eddie was supposed to ring the bells when the chalice was raised to its highest point by Father Patterson. He threw in a few more rings for good measure. What harm could that do? And the fact that Father Patterson had to tell us it was time to grab the patens (a sacred plate with a handle that was held under a person's chin in case the communion was dropped.) was very incidental. After all, we had only done this service for the past four years. Anybody could forget a tough detail like that. I personally thought the service went quite well. I think Father Patterson had other feelings.

When he finally addressed the congregation and told them to "Go in peace," we all turned to go back to the tabernacle, all of us that is except for Eddie who just stood there as he watched the congregation leave the church. His back was to Father and me. Father looked down at me and said, "Go get your brother."

I walked back out to the altar and gently grabbed Eddie by the elbow to guide him back. We slipped our cassocks off by pulling them over our heads, and instead of hanging our garb on separate hangers, I hung mine right over Eddie's. I wasn't sure why, but it looked good that way. Why waste a hanger. We tried to get out of there in a hurried fashion, and we thought we had executed the perfect plan, until we were about to leave. "Boys," I heard Father Patterson say in a stern voice, "next time you decide to drink wine, do it after the service okay?"

I didn't know what to say. With any kind of denial, marching straight to the confessional would have been in order. Eddie didn't say a word; he was just looking at his shoes. I was thinking more on terms of what was going to happen to us when Mom found out.

All I could say was, "Okay." It was an admission of what we did, but at the same time, it didn't seem so bad. At least Father wasn't yelling at us, but I'm sure he wanted to hear some guilt in our voices at our next confession and maybe some details of our misconduct.

We shuffled out of the church and walked toward our bikes. I could hear Father raise his voice as he stood in the doorway, "I know you boys know the difference between right and wrong, and sometimes the wrong thing is more fun, but the wrong thing almost always has consequences. If it happens again, I *will* tell your mother." I knew he was doing us a favor because the last thing we needed was for our mother to find out. From that day forward whenever I thought of the word "cool" to describe a person, I thought of Father Patterson. That was the first and the last time I drank wine in the church basement, before mass anyway.

8

We were half way there so getting to LaCrosse around noon was a real possibility. Now that we had enough gas, oil, and snacks from the gas station, we were good to go. Mary had the radio tuned to 89 AM WLS out of Chicago, *Where the Hits Just Keep on Coming.* Terry Jacks was singing "Seasons in the Sun."

"I really like this song," she said.

"Yeah, it's a good one alright," I agreed.

"I can't wait for his next hit," she added.

"Hey Mom, did you bring the paper with us?" I asked.

"Yeah, it's around here somewhere. Look around," she said, as she pointed toward the backseat. I twisted, looked over the seat, and saw it lying on the floor…

1971…I dashed out of the door hopping with bare feet through this windowed freezer. I snapped up the news in the form of *The Wisconsin State Journal* from my front porch. My breath was jutting out making its appearance. I quickly pivoted and flew back through the front door where the warmth encased me. I slyly thought to myself, *I'll bet Trazzini couldn't get the paper that fast.* The cold winter had everyone anxious for spring. I was a sophomore at Lake Mills High School and part of a state-ranked wrestling team. It was five A.M. in the morning, and I was trying very hard to shake the morning feeling out of my head. My first thought when I got up was, *In 48 hours, it will all be over.* This spiral wad of paper almost had a life of its own. *The Journal* was wrapped with a red rubber band around it. The information that lay inside beckoned me. I loved the attention wrestling gave me, but previous issues had a sportswriter from the paper add an extra ingredient to spice up the possible bout between myself and McFarland's Bill Trazzini. He made the match sound like the upcoming fight between Ali and Frasier. Of course, this could have been how I saw it. At first, I was honored to be put in the same light as Trazzini. It made me wonder why I was even considered a threat to him. After all, he was a two time state qualifier, while I was only a conference champ. The writer went on to say we were made from the same mold. That alone made me ooze with confidence. Who was I to argue with this expert sportswriter? He said we were both short, strong and had bodies that were ready to unleash a wide variety of moves. The fact that I had two older brothers to toughen me up (much to their pleasure) was not even an advantage. Trazzini had a long history of wrestling in his blood. He also had brothers that probably put him through the same regiment of pain. The ultimate match had been played in my head a thousand times. Visualizing a victory was the first step in the right direction.

I was just two feet inside the door, and I sat on my haunches. I quickly discarded anything that didn't resemble the "peach sheet." *The Journal* always had the sports section typed on peach-colored paper. As I ravaged through the rag, I felt possessed. The paper began to look like someone just unpacked a house full of dishes. I breezed through the sports page missing everything. The second time through I focused, and page four revealed the treasure. The headlines read, "**Stoughton-McFarland to Dominate Regionals.**"

All year, Stoughton was in the top three in the High School Wrestling Rankings. They destroyed many teams in their wake, Lake Mills included. One of the few losses I had all year was to a tall, lanky Stoughton Viking grappler with the same last name. Doug Davis was a head taller than me, and he looked like a skeleton with skin and skills. I weighed 92 pounds soaking wet, and if I hadn't seen him weigh in, I would never have believed he was 98 pounds. Stoughton blood flowed through him, so he probably enrolled in mandatory wrestling camp at birth. With his gangly appearance and reach, it made me think of him as the superhero Spiderman. It was impossible to get away from him when he sprawled on top of you with his long legs and arms.

Our earlier dual match took place in Madison. It was the only time in my brief career that the final score had me confused. The tie match should have been indicated by the referee raising both of our arms at the conclusion. When only Doug's arm was raised, I thought there had been a mistake. I stood in the middle of the mat waiting for them to correct their error. I flipped my head to the scoreboard to see the dreadful final score, 1-0. My heart was jammed in my throat. My insides screamed with humiliation. The rest of the team didn't do well either. I felt oddly like one of the Lake Mills losers that day. Our team was simply crushed by a dynasty.

"Remember how you feel," Assistant Coach Kelly said, "win big and you'll never have to be surprised by the score." He patted me on my head sympathetically, like I was a toddler. That loss and his advice had a major impact on me. Seven matches and seven wins later, I tried not to forget how frustrating that feeling was.

Today was different because this was Regionals. As I boarded the bus at eight A.M., Head Coach Lipske and the rest of the team were settling in when Coach Kelly made his way toward my seat. *Please don't talk to me, I'm too nervous,* I thought.

Coach Kelly was a stout, strong man. He was fresh out of college, and he had the attitude to prove it. He had dark, short hair, and his round face was accented with black rimmed glasses that constantly slid down his nose. He would always look over his glasses as he talked to you. His voice was always hoarse; this time wasn't any different. "Slide over, Davis," he piped. "Listen; forget about all the crap you read in the paper. Just take one match at a time. You got that?" He grabbed my shoulder and waited for a response.

"Okay Coach," I said in almost a whisper. He got up, lumbered to the front of the bus, and plopped down next to Coach Lipske. Coach Lipske was the technical part of the wrestling equation, while Coach Kelly was the motivator. Kelly had a way to read the kids and get to the core. I loved both coaches' admiration for their kids. Lipske and Kelly were both wrestling stock and loved the sport. Both were barrel-chested and powerful. Fortunately, for the guys below 150 pounds, we never had to deal with the punishment like they put on the upper weights during practice. The respect we felt for these coaches brought on the will to win which was evident by our success; Stoughton being the exception.

Butterflies did a waltz in my stomach as we approached the regional sight, Stoughton. It occurred to me on our trek that the possibility was very real that I would have to do battle with not only Trazzini, but Doug Davis as well. To survive that would be brutal.

One match at a time, slammed through my brain. The pairings were listed on a small cardboard bracket hanging in the hallway. Wrestlers were gathering at their appropriate brackets like cattle at feeding time. The 98 pound bracket was easy to spot with Doug Davis' height dwarfing the competition. As I made my way, I slid through bodies to inspect the pairings. I came nose to nose with Bill Trazzini. It was the first time I actually saw him, and his body lived up to the billing. *A rock with legs,* I mused to myself. My many years of churchgoing paid off because he was in the opposite bracket along with Davis. The program listed him with one loss. I could only imagine what the savage looked like that got the best of him.

My quest slowly took shape as I handled my first opponent from Jefferson. I knew my next competition was a scrappy wrestler when he took me down immediately. Spencer from Platteville was a seasoned, strong kid. It was as though someone stuck a smelling salt under my nose and brought me back to life. I quickly reversed him as I heard a roar from the Stoughton crowd. I noticed Doug Davis was wrestling Trazzini on the other mat. I had all I could do to concentrate on my own match. I wanted to be a spectator at that point and watch that war. The waves of cheers that were being created by the action on the other mat had my mind racing. I simply had to bear down and get myself into my own match.

One match at time, I kept telling myself. Like a bear out of hibernation, I tore into Spencer. As time ran out, his season was one loss away from ending. He knew he was lucky to score a takedown. I still couldn't understand the huge ovation that occurred when the referee raised my arm. I then realized the bedlam was for the other Davis, Doug.

The impossible had happened. The mighty Bill Trazzini was upset by Spiderman. Trazzini stood in shock as Doug leapt into the arms of his coach. The partisan crowd was hysterical. The stage was set for the match of my career. The next morning, the peach sheet said that Davis would win. They couldn't be wrong with that prediction since two Davis's were to meet in the finals. With every breath, my body felt like it was packed with springs and the slightest cut would expel an explosion of flying shrapnel.

Poor Spencer from Platteville, he had the misfortune of facing Trazzini in the consolation bracket. Trazzini's only hope to advance to next week's tournament rode on my loss to Doug Davis and his win over Spencer. He would then have to face me, and he would have to win. He dismantled Spencer, disposing of him in less than two minutes. He finished Spencer's season with an exclamation point.

Our match was next, and the Stoughton gym was packed to the brim with kids and adult spectators. My heart was racing. I was sweating, and yet I was chilled. The mat that hosted the championship bout was unaware that it was about to absorb a battle. A battle that would be retold and written about by anyone present that wanted to recall a wrestling classic.

Doug Davis sprang to the mat as he was introduced by the tournament voice. The color in the announcer's voice turned fluorescent for the occasion.

"From Stoughton…with a record of 21 and 7...Doug... DAAAVIS!" boomed the voice. With a black singlet and the traditional **Stoughton** slashed across his chest, Doug juked and stutter-stepped to the center of the mat, waiting to catch his prey. "From Lake Mills…with a record of 20 and 5…Pat DAAAVIS!" bellowed the speaker. The white ***L-Cat*** embroidered on the top half of my singlet matched the color of the pound of cotton gathering in my mouth. I hopped to the center of the mat and shook my arms, trying to stay loose. The ref in the zebra shirt made his way to the dueling Davis boys.

"Shake hands," he barked. My forward motion was met by a long limb that resembled the front leg of a spider. Doug never advanced to honor the zebra's request; he simply swung his arm out in my direction as we shook hands. *Only a mortician could feel a hand that cold,* I thought. His hand was like ice.

The shrill blast of the referee's whistle unleashed the action. The sounds of the cheers were regulated like a child in control of a volume knob, loud, soft, loud, soft…Every time one of us came close to a takedown, the volume was turned up. Doug's leverage fought off my every attack. My strength crushed his advances. The first two minutes ended with defense, and the scoreboard rang true, 0-0.

My arms felt like granite. I shook them to get some life into them. One period was history, and there were two to go. My tongue was welded in my mouth. The short stocky referee was sweating almost as much as we were. He flipped the green and red disk into orbit. Upon contact, the side of the disk hit the mat making it roll in a small circle. It finally ran out of gas and lay with the green side up. The same color as my leg band. The stout zebra pointed to me, indicating that I had choice of position. My choice could only be shown by a gesture. My mouth voiced down, but the motion of my thumb made the ref understand. My mouth was useless, except to pull in huge gulps of air. Four more minutes of this seemed like an eternity. As I got on all fours, Spiderman wrapped my waste with his web-like grip. The pop of the zebra's whistle started the clock. I was on a fishing line trying to elude the angler, only to be reeled in. Every attempt was thwarted by his length. Finally, his six pound test line was snapped by my eight pounds of desire.

"ESCAPE, ONE!" yelled the ref. He was barely heard over the crowd, but the sound was music to my ears. Doug's shock of my escape made him charge me like a bully on the playground. I dodged him easily as he advanced again. It was almost comical. Obviously, the referee wasn't laughing, as he screamed with the whistle clamped between his teeth, "WARNING GREEN, STALLING!" He was pointing to me, as though I didn't know where the middle of the mat was. Suddenly, the glorious sound of the buzzer ended the second round. The scoreboard by the clock read: GREEN-1 RED-0.

My life on this mat only had to last two more minutes, I thought. The chant of: "DAVIS, DAVIS, DAVIS," erupted throughout the building. I looked up into the crowd to see my mom and dad leading the cheer. Fists were thrusting in the air, and the crowd actually had an angry look on their faces. The atmosphere was intense, and I had to convince myself that the cheer was for me and not Doug, although the Stoughton crowd was yelling as loud as anyone. Revenge would be mine if the score stayed the same for the next two minutes. My arms were showing signs of the battle. There were bruises and small red lines that mapped the tears of flesh along the length of both arms. I could taste blood in my mouth. It was a familiar sign I knew all too well. My chest was heaving with every breath, and I felt like my lungs were on fire.

Doug took the down position with zeal. I wondered where he got all his energy. I slowly wrapped my arm around his thin waist. The whistle started the last 120 seconds. I struggled to hang onto this elusive snake. My ability to try to turn him on his back was absent. I could only concentrate on countering his every attempt to escape. "GET MOVING GREEN!" snapped the zebra.

Only seconds later, the ref yelled, "WARNING GREEN, STALLING!" I knew then, one more stalling call on me would give Spiderman a point and a tie. The chances of me turning this bag of bones over was about the same as me spitting, none. "*TWENTY FOUR MORE SECONDS, NINETEEN SECONDS, FIFTEEN, TWELVE,*" I counted silently.

"ONE POINT RED, GREEN STALLING!" screamed the whistle-mouthed ref. The Stoughton crowd went nuts! The buzzer should have ended this marathon, but the striped-clad man extended the finish line. I squinted to confirm the tally. The floor level scoreboard displayed: GREEN-1 RED-1. The insane spectators were getting their money's worth with an additional three-minute encore. I now had an idea what the gladiators felt like in Rome. A three-minute overtime was not what I wanted, and by the looks of Doug Davis, he knew he had a whole new lease on life.

9

A strobe light flickered in my head, and my body followed the small dots to the edge of the mat. Now, black spots filled my sight as I gasped for air. Both hands held my hips, and my shoulders heaved up and down with every breath. The weight of Coach Kelly's hand on my shoulder felt like he was pushing rather than touching. Coach Lipske sprayed water towards my mouth. The line that resembled my lips did not open in time. The stream splashed my face, and that glorious solution melted the lock. I was able to open my mouth as the second blast exploded in my throat. My tongue came to life. My arms sprang out and guided the water bottle to my mouth. I gave a quick look at the clock that was counting down the end of our small break. Thirty-eight seconds clicked in time with the crowd clapping in rhythm. Coach Kelly was on one knee looking me directly in the eye as I turned away from the clock. His white dress shirt was soaked around the collar, and his tie was loosened up a quarter ways down his shirt. With every other word he spoke, he used his index finger to keep his glasses on his nose.

He ordered hoarsely, "Listen to me! Listen! Think about two things, Mr. Davis." He only used "Mr." when he wanted your undivided attention. "One, think about what it felt like the last time you lost to this guy! Two, take a quick look over there," his head motioned over toward Trazzini. Trazzini stood with his arms crossed staring straight through me. "You don't win here...you deal with *that!*" He didn't have to spell it out. I knew what he meant.

"DAVIS, DAVIS, DAVIS!" came from the bleachers.

"Be aggressive," he said, "or the ref will call stalling again!"

"Kay," my voice cracked.

The sound of the buzzer ended our brief break. Doug was already waiting for me in the middle of the mat. I shuffled over to continue the melee. We slapped hands for a token handshake. The two-legged zebra voiced a whistle to begin the motion. As I circled, I noticed dried blood crusting around Doug's nostrils. His long black hair protruded out of his headgear that was taking the shape of horns. He looked as tired as I felt. One of his white socks was yanked down and was half covering the red band around his ankle. The red ring teased me. My timing had to be just right to make my attack effective.

His shoulder and bicep crushed my brow as I shot deep into his ankle. My eyes burned from the salty sweat of his skin as he grunted with resistance. Once again, his leverage was holding off my strength. *Ten more seconds and I would gain control.* The shriek of a buzzer would put an end to the first period with no score. A glimmer of faint success regenerated some energy I didn't know existed, and confidence filled my soul. With a flip of the ref's wrist, the green-red disk flew into the air. Even the disk was running on low. It didn't want to go through the motion of landing on its side and rolling around in circles. It landed flat with a plop. The color again was green. The zebra looked at me; I motioned down. Doug encased me with his long, thin arm. The ref whistled, and I exploded up struggling to escape the sticky clutches of my Viking foe. His determination was evident with every grunt and sigh. Thirty-five seconds to escape beamed the clock. I stood up quickly and tried to face him, only to be tripped by his vine- like legs. There were small, red skid marks of blood marking the mat where my elbows just landed. Nine seconds of pure expulsion flew out of me as I made one last desperate effort to free myself. Spiderman wrapped me up as we both crashed to the floor as time ran out.

A timeout was called as the Stoughton coach crammed cotton in Doug's nostrils. The damage came when we hit the mat. I could feel his nose hit the back of my head. Droplets of blood were toweled off the battleground before the last stanza began. Concrete flowed through my veins as I tried to move my arms.

The light familiar sound of my mother's voice penetrated the rest of the crowd. "Come on, Pat...You can do it," she screamed. At this point, all I wanted to do was to wake up from this nightmare. My confidence waned because I knew Doug truly had the advantage. The score still read 0-0, but the idea of holding him down for sixty seconds didn't seem remotely possible. Even if I did contain him, the Viking warrior would win. I just had too many stalling penalties called on me during regulation. A tie was a loss, and Trazzini was warming up on the sidelines. His coach was talking to him in his ear while pointing toward our match.

Doug crouched in the down position to begin the last leg of this bruising epic. The ref clenched the whistle in his teeth and signaled me to assume the top spot. The smell of raw perspiration filled the air. The twang of the whistle blew through my head, and with no resistance, Spiderman bulleted forward and flew from my grip. I simply let him go to a 1-0 deficit. That was the easiest part of my plan. The real challenge was about to begin. I had to attack him and take him down. I knew it was a long shot, since I had never been able to take him down, but it was my only hope. I advanced cautiously as he defended his lead. Doug quickly back peddled off the mat.

The man in stripes immediately yelled, "STAY ON THE MAT RED!" as he pointed to the Viking grappler. *Forty-eight seconds left.* I charged again, hooking his ankle. I hung on to it as I tried to lift it. Doug's long arm bashed my forehead once again with a strong force across my face. This time the pain felt good. The blow was hard enough to spark a fire in my gut. He strategically positioned himself off the mat. The zebra blew his instrument. "WARNING, STALLING RED!" he barked. *TWENTY-SEVEN* ticks away said the orange digital clock: RED-1 GREEN-0.

The plugs in Doug's nose showed solid red. He was pulling in oxygen while his chest grew large and then small. The taste of blood flowed through my teeth. Trazzini rolled his head in circular motions, trying to loosen up.

I quickly glanced at Kelly. One index finger was holding his glasses up while the other hand was clenched in a fist. I could see him yelling, "GET HIM!" The sound of his voice was lost with the crowd. The bout resumed with the sound of the whistle. The red spiral on the black spider's leg stood out. *NINETEEN, EIGHTEEN,* clicked the orange display. The red ring kept its distance. My life was being drained by an electronic timer. *FOURTEEN, THIRTEEN,* my body became steel and the red strap on the Viking's ankle became a magnet. Speed and determination sunk deep into Spiderman's defenses. Both of my arms encompassed Doug's leg. He grunted with all the strength he had and tried to force me off for the last *TEN SECONDS.* The sold-out gym expelled a solid sound. The sight of blood splotches smeared the mat. The sources were many, but specifically unknown. His gangly leverage was overcome by the strength of my determination and the fear of Trazzini. I covered him and grabbed his waist with what I had left in my tank. I was on fumes.

"TWO, TAKEDOWN, GREEN!" screamed the ref, who was holding up two fingers while pointing at me. The blast of the horn was the foot that crushed the spider. White towels wrapped in athletic tape were flying in the air (a ritual often used when the crowd noise overwhelms the buzzer), targeting the zebra, to indicate the war was over. The noise was deafening. The zebra's cheeks puffed out as he pulled us apart. His whistle was blowing, but the bedlam was winning. My worthy foe rolled on his back and stared at the lights in pure exhaustion. His arms lay straight out at his side like a tinker-toy man. I stumbled to my feet and was visited by flashing black spots again. Both palms clutched my knees as I tried to overcome the feeling of fatigue that surrounded me. With one last ounce of energy, I was able to swivel my head toward the scoreboard to confirm the victory: GREEN-2 RED-1. The man in black and white took my wrist and led me over to the fallen Viking. While holding onto me, he flung his arm out to assist the sprawled mass. We looked like two children being led to detention after a playground fight. We were guided to the center of the mat. Our arms weakly found each others hands as we shook to finalize the match. Without thinking, we both simultaneously raised our arms and patted each other on the shoulder saying, "Good match." It was a gesture of mutual respect. The ref raised my arm while holding onto my wrist. My eyes shot over to Trazzini. He had his head buried in his knees as he sat on the floor. His hope for advancement ended with the sound of the buzzer. Many times I had battled him in my mind, but no imaginary match could compare to the one that just took place. To meet him on the mat would only happen where it began…in my mind.

However, my imagination could not reserve room for something that wouldn't be. It was only vacant for possibilities. Next week, a wrestler from Janesville Craig would end my quest to wrestle at the state level. Ned Towns was his name, and his future would make him an All-American. His school's mascot was a Cougar, and it fit his demeanor on the mat. He knew he had a creditable opponent, but this was one beast I could not tame.

10

"Don't forget to send Grandpa a birthday card, Pat," my mom said, as she lit a cigarette.

"I won't. I grabbed a card from home to send him when I get to school," I quickly responded.

"How old is he going to be?" Mary asked.

"Seventy-six," Mom and I said together.

"I think I am going to send him some of those chattering teeth," I said laughing.

"He loves that kind of stuff," Mom said with the cigarette hanging from her lip.

"I can just see him showing everybody the teeth and laughing like crazy," Mary added.

"I think he wore out the small laughing box I got him last year," Mom said.

"I wouldn't doubt it," I said, "You're lucky to have him as a dad."

"You're lucky to have him as a grandpa," Mom said seriously.

Mary and I both said, "Yeah." We knew she was right. He was a one of a kind person. He could tease you to tears, and five minutes later, he would make you feel like a million bucks. One of the most important values he taught me was to be generous. He continually gave of himself and never really asked for anything in return except gratitude. Accepting anything from him and not being grateful was a quick way of getting on his bad side.

We all learned that lesson at an early age. Some of us learned the lesson much to his pleasure...

Grandpa did not have very much money, but when we were with him, we felt rich. He taught me many things, but the most important one was that money doesn't make someone rich; it's the substance of one's character that does. He was the kind of person that you wanted to be around all the time because what ever he did or said mattered. He had a zest for life; everyone he knew was touched by his spirit and generosity. To this day, the same excitement rushes to my heart when I think of his visits. Living in southern Wisconsin, I am not too far away from where Grandpa grew up. When he was young, his father gathered his family and moved to south Chicago where work was a little more plentiful. I knew that my Grandpa's visits were trips that brought him back home. Even when I was quite young, I could see this in his eyes. When he sat outside on our picnic table, he would often inhale the air and take in the state he lived in as a youth. He loved the big oak trees and the deep blue lakes in Wisconsin.

He worked in a foundry that made railroad parts, and by the look of his forearms, he forged every part the Chicago and Northwestern Railroad ever used. He was a man of substance and brawn. His height was a mere five foot six, but he weighed close to 220 pounds. Now a normal man of that size would seem overweight, but he definitely was not that. He was a proud German who walked with a swagger. He sported very little hair and had no teeth at all, but that didn't hold him back from eating a steak and showing off a big smile. He chewed snuff and had a can to spit in no matter where he sat, his truck included. God forbid if you accidentally kicked over his Butternut spit can. I would rather clean a hundred fish than to take on that clean up duty. That's probably why we always piled in the back of his pickup truck any time we went somewhere with him. He spent at least two weeks of vacation in Wisconsin every summer, and those weeks were the best two weeks of the year. Fishing was the first priority for him. Eddie (named after Grandpa) and I would pick night crawlers a few days in advance to be properly prepared. I remember more times than not picking worms in my pajamas. I think it was easier for my mom to have us get ready for bed before we caught our bait. It could have been our idea too. That way we could stay out a little later. Heck, we just had to wash our hands and jump into bed. Who wouldn't agree with that theory? One part of our refrigerator was reserved for night crawlers. Mom made all of us aware that the cottage cheese container was designated for that purpose. Every once in a while someone would accidentally open a container of worms and the sound of their dismay would be the delight of everyone else. It was usually Claudia that fell prey to that mistake.

Fishing with Grandpa was great, but there was one small drawback, the getting up at 5 A.M. part. After several trips to the lake, I really had to know why we had to get up that early. What he told me made perfect sense. "If we got out on the lake early enough, we wouldn't wake the fish. The last thing we wanted to do was to scare them away." I guess the fish had all the luck. We had to get up in the dark, and they got to sleep in. I changed my thoughts on the fish's luck as soon as we started to haul them in. We kept every bluegill we caught. When we asked why we kept even the little ones, his response would be, "Dems good eatin'."

Grandpa would load the cane poles in the back of his pickup truck while Eddie and I would grab the worms and stagger toward his truck trying to shake the sleep from our bodies. Sure we were tired, but it wouldn't be long after that that we would have plenty of energy. A few bottles of pop and a handful of candy bars would do that to a kid. Of course, Grandpa had plenty of energy to burn by the time we got up. The way he drank coffee out of a quart bowl with plenty of milk and sugar would put an extra hop in anyone's step. Probably the same reason goes for him never wanting to rent a motor with his boat. Rowing seemed effortless for him. Eddie and I were in charge of the anchors, one in front and one in back. You could bet on his words of warning every time we were about to throw the lead balls over the side: "Make sure the God damn rope is tied to the anchor." By the tone of his voice, he paid for a few anchors in his past.

After fishing for a few hours, we knew when it was time to go home. Either our stringer was full, or Grandpa had exhausted his share of stories. Most of his stories we had heard already several times, but that didn't take away the thrill of hearing them again. He used colorful words to describe the many adventures and shenanigans that painted his past. Words like God Damn, Jesus Christ and Son of a Bitch come to mind. All of his stories were told in the same manner. He started out serious, and by the time he got half way through, he would be holding back a laugh. The ending would build with him laughing so hard you could hardly understand what he was saying. Anytime he told a new story, you better hope you were near someone that heard it already, so they could interpret his last few sentences and relay the punch line on to you. Most of the time, we all knew what he was saying, the fact that he told the same stories a thousand times helped. His accumulation of most stories was from past visits and the trouble us kids got into while he was here. This summer wouldn't be any different. While he was here, we were bound to act-up and get in trouble. Exorbitant amounts of sugar would speed that process along. Temporary hyper-insanity is the technical term for it. Okay, that's my term, but it's fitting. Obviously, besides taking a dip of snuff, Grandpa's real vice was sugar. I could say he had a tremendous sweet tooth, but you have to have at least one tooth for that. He gave up another vice years ago. According to Mom, he stopped drinking when he was in his forties. If he drank alcohol the way he put down soda, I could see why he quit. It was a mission for Eddie and me to try to keep up with him when it came to knocking down cream soda and grape Nehi.

The competition was close when we were at home, but our little bladders lost when it came to drinking in the boat. We knew we were going to catch hell when we had to tell the old man we had to take a leak ten minutes into the fishing trip. Soon, soda was off limits on fishing trips that involved a boat. We were relegated to Charleston Chews and Baby Ruth bars. It didn't matter though because we had plenty of soda to drink when we got home. We never had soda or any other sweets around the house until Grandpa visited. Our teeth suffered because of it. It was rumored at one time that our dentist set up an open account in my Grandpa's name. I'm positive the amount of money my folks shelled out to the dentist could have paid for his family vacations.

The first order of business when Grandpa arrived was to get supplies. It was a euphoric feeling watching him grab cases of soda, loads of candy, and other off limit pleasures we weren't spoiled with during the year. On one of his visits, there were three cases of soda sitting on the porch just calling our name. All it took was a summer thirst and no one around to tell us what our limit was. We knew what our limit was, but like a drunk, once we got a taste, we couldn't get enough, especially when no one was around to guard the treasure.

Grandpa was going to the bakery to visit with his old pal Ernie, and then he was going to try his luck fishing alone. Mom was helping Dad because Ernie was next to useless when Grandpa was around. The rest of the kids were off doing the normal summer stuff. It was around ten in the morning, and Eddie and I knew he wouldn't be back until noon. Two hours was a lifetime away to wait for permission to have some pop. We decided we needed to try a cream soda. We just had to see if they changed the glorious taste from the last time we had it, exactly one summer ago. You just never know; the soda industry is funny that way. They make a product that we all like and suddenly they change the taste. We just had to make sure that wasn't happening. We started out by opening one bottle and sharing it. We were sure Grandpa wouldn't mind that. Shortly after, we convinced ourselves that there may have been a slight difference in the taste compared to last year. Only another sampling could prove our theory. A half a bottle would never be enough to positively tell. Any professional "soda taste tester" could tell you that you need large volumes of soda to make an accurate assessment. After three and one half bottles a piece, we forgot why we were drinking so much. We were like dogs rolling in crap. It wasn't enough to drink the soda we had, but we had to shake up a few bottles and spray each other. We were totally out of control. The scene must have looked like a two person World Series celebration. When Eddie and I came to our senses, there were caps and empty bottles lying all over the place. That wasn't a problem though; we knew at our ripe old ages (eight and nine) that all we had to do was to put the bottles back into the wooden case and no one would know the difference.

Noon passed, and Grandpa came home with a stringer of fish. He immediately asked who wanted to help him clean them. The fact that he threw in that there would be a reward for some help made Eddie and I volunteer right away. We strung out the garden hose and retrieved the five gallon bucket from our shed. The bucket was one thing around our house that was always put back, and we knew where to look for it. It was the same bucket that carried tons of fish remains to their final resting place, our garden. It was my turn to scale, and Eddie's turn to gut the fish. He threw the guts and heads into the bucket. Occasionally, a small crayfish would be found as we did the autopsy. Cleaning fish gave us an idea of what we looked like inside, in most cases minus the crayfish. We had at least a dozen cleaned when our cat Pierre decided that all of our labor was giving her an appetite. She was observing the whole process from our picnic table. An occasional scale would fly and land on her head, but she paid no attention to that. She jumped from the table and stuck her head, deep into the bucket. She wanted some of that wonderful mess. Eddie helped her need by throwing a handful of remains on the ground. She wolfed it down like she hadn't eaten for a week. We couldn't believe any animal would eat anything so disgusting. We finished just in time for lunch as Mom called us in to eat.

Eddie and I washed our hands as Grandpa started to fry the fish. Mom asked us about our day, and we just told her the usual answer. We played ball and rode bikes. The soda incident was only a few hours in our past, but for some reason we conveniently forgot to tell her about that. Lunch was ready, and as we began to eat, Pierre waltzed into the kitchen from outside. Mom commented that perhaps the cat was pregnant again because her belly was showing signs. We were clueless as to what she was referring to when we saw that her belly was almost dragging on the ground. I didn't know anything about the pregnancy thing, but I was almost positive that a cat couldn't get pregnant by eating fish guts. I would have to ask the neighborhood expert, Oz, about that later. He always gave us all the information we asked for and sometimes information we didn't need to know. Once he told me how babies got inside a mother's stomach. I knew then he stretched the truth because there was no way my dad and mom would do that. Suddenly, Pierre gave the patented cat hurl warning. The action I am talking about can only be described as "Oooopa, Oooopa, Oooopa." The motion itself looks like a cat is trying to retrieve a toy he or she swallowed that is lodged deep within its belly. Only this time it was not a toy, but something that should have been buried along with the rest of the remains. Too often we had seen Pierre go through this routine but what came next would be a first. It was the first and only time I ever saw a cat vomit on its hind legs. She literally sat up and projected a pound of fish guts all over the floor.

"OH MY GOD!" Mom yelled. As a kid, things like that were hysterical. Eddie and I cracked up immediately and continued to laugh until Mom told us that we had to clean it up. That took the humor right out of the situation. Grandpa stayed calm at the stove and made the comment that perhaps Pierre wasn't pregnant. I was thinking if she was pregnant, she just gave birth to an alien. Lunch ended and we hovered around Grandpa because his next move was so predictable.

He would sit on the couch, rub the stubble on his face, look into the distance, and say, "Boy, that fish sure made me dry."

We knew this meant one thing. It was close to "soda time." Grandpa got up, walked to the porch, and returned with a bottle of orange. That was strange because he normally carried enough back for everyone. In this case, he sat back on the couch, took a long drink, and gave out a resounding, "AAaahh!" Eddie and I just stared back at him and asked him if we could have some too.

Without even a hesitation, he nodded and said with a slight smirk, "Sure, go ahead boys, have all you want." Eddie and I smartly marched to the back porch to fill our soda need. We soon discovered that the magical, carbonated, colored liquid was not there. The explanation was simple, there had to have been a robbery. We trotted back to tell Grandpa the sad news.

"Grandpa, Grandpa, all the soda is gone!"

"No it's not! It's back there," he said confidently.

"Where?"

"Back there," he said pointing toward the back porch.

"All your soda is in the backyard lying in the grass and on the ground; that's where your soda is boys," he said almost laughing, like he was enjoying the lesson he was teaching us.

We knew exactly what he was talking about.

We both walked away with our heads down, only to hear him say with some sarcasm in his voice, "Shake up some more soda, boys, waste it all…hahaha…spill it all over the ground...who cares…Grandpa will buy more… hahahaha."

It was a tough lesson to learn, but our soda drinking days were over for at least this trip. Eddie and I sulked in our backyard. We tried to figure out how he found out, but at that point, it didn't matter; we were soda-less. We were wondering if the A&W Root Beer Stand was going to be off limits too. After a day of guilt, and constant reminders of how much we wasted, Grandpa finally broke down and took us to the root beer stand for a cone. We felt lucky to even get that with how we behaved. We learned a valuable lesson that day, but the wrath of his teasing and constant reminder of how foolish we were was something I didn't want to go through again. A summer visit from him couldn't go by without him mentioning the time Eddie and I wasted several bottles of pop. Over the years, the story was told with the same style. Of course, we had to interpret the last few sentences to our younger cousins hearing it for the first time because it was impossible to understand him through his laughter.

11

The road seemed endless as we weaved and turned through the bluffs and the hills of western Wisconsin. I normally enjoyed the scenery, but I was too preoccupied in thought. I knew in the back of my mind that college was a long-shot. I really didn't like school enough to go four more years, but I felt I had to give it a chance. I looked up and saw the green road sign: **Viroqua 25 Miles.** I looked at my map, and I could see that we were making some progress. I felt like once I got to LaCrosse, I could get on with my life. Sitting in this car was suspending me from my future. Mary played with the radio, trying to rid it of its static.

"It's the hills, Honey," Mom told her, "wait until we get in a flat area." Mary just huffed and turned the radio down to a whisper. You could hear the soft sound of the music but with a slight crackle.

"Crocodile Rock" was fading out as the DJ let everyone know, "That was Elton John as he rocks with the crocodiles."

"Huh, Elton...John…I didn't know he sang that song," I said sarcastically.

Mary looked up at me from the corner of her eye with a slight smile and said, "Yeah, right."

Mom kept her eyes on the road as she maneuvered the curves. A lit cigarette was lying in the ashtray as both hands firmly held the steering wheel. Mom wasn't very tall, and she always drove like she was trying to find a penny on the road. She was slightly hunched and attentive as she studied the asphalt. We came into a clearing, and Mary fiddled with the volume knob again. The next song came in pure and clean. B.W. Stevenson was inside the little glowing box that indicated 89. He was singing "My Maria." It was a catchy tune that continually went back to the chorus. I could see Mary mouthing the words, and Mom's hand was tapping to the rhythm. I cracked the window slightly to get rid of some of the smoke from the cigarette still resting at an angle in the ashtray...

1966..."Here...take 'em. Don't get them wet. I'll meet you under the porch," Oz said in a whisper. He dropped the three cigarettes he had stolen from his dad into my hand and quickly slammed the window closed as he peered down at Tommy and me. Like many of the neighbors, Tommy was at our house so much, he's like part of our family.

It was January, and I was a month away from turning eleven. Our breath was visible as we plotted in our mischievous way. The small space under Oz's porch was a perfect place for smoking .The broken lattice made a hole just big enough to allow a kid with cigarettes through.

"Don't crush them," Tommy said in a loud whisper.

As I crawled through the small wooden, oblong hole under the porch, I could hear Tommy warning me again, "Be careful with the weeds!"

We both laughed because just recently we had heard that expression for the first time and were just waiting for the right opportunity to use it. He beat me to the punch as we both tried to contain our: *No laughing in church giggle* because we were in that same type of situation. I struggled to get under the porch. It was harder this time of year because of our many layers of clothing. The jagged wood kept snagging my coat and resisting my entrance. I freed myself as Tommy pushed my feet through the hole. He followed quickly behind me. We huddled on the frozen dirt as we removed our gloves.

"Got matches?" he asked.

"Yeah," I said, "we better wait till Oz comes."

"Alright," Tommy agreed. "Jeez, it's cold down here."

"It has to be cold, so when they see the smoke they'll think it's just our breath," I said, like I was trying to teach him something.

"Yeah, yeah, good thinking," Tommy said as his teeth chattered. "Where the hell is he?" he said laughing again.

Swearing was funny, and we did it more or less to *be* funny. We didn't dare swear around our parents, so we had to make up for lost time when we were away. Swearing was like a tennis match at our age. Once someone started the volley of words, it went until our attention was altered or an adult was in sight. It made for cheap entertainment anyway.

"Yeah, where the HELL is he?" I asked, like I had a speech problem. I knew that would get Tommy going. His snicker turned into a belly laugh almost immediately. I kept laughing while telling him to be quiet.

"Five more minutes we'll wait," I said.

"If he doesn't come soon, we'll freeze to death. In April they'll find two rotting piles of smell under this porch," Tommy said with a chattering voice as he breathed into his cupped hands.

"Yep," I agreed with Tommy, but I followed up in my animated voice again, "I can just hear Oz... as he looks at our dead bodies saying, 'I told them not to smoke.'"

"Yeah, no shit," Tommy said chuckling a bit.

Only recently, I had discovered that Oz was not his real name. It was like any other nickname in the neighborhood. Once labeled with it, you were stuck with it. He is two years older than me and four over Tommy. I once heard my mom say that Oz was too mature for his age. She must have been talking about his size. He outweighed Tommy and I put together, and he was at least a foot taller. Why we hung around him is a mystery. Almost everything we did with Oz got us in trouble, but he had a way of making us believe that everything we did was necessary.

My first experience of trouble should have given me a clue that he was a thunderstorm wrapped inside a boy's body. When Eddie and I were five and six, Oz convinced us that he had a club. The only way we could be in his club was to be nude. His clubhouse was a refrigerator box placed in his backyard, tucked deep into bushes that lined his property. The initiation was to enter the box, throw our clothes outside through a window, and wait until Oz brought them back. That's how Eddie and I understood it anyway. We must have misunderstood him because after we threw our clothes out, Oz scooped them up and ran inside the house with them. We stayed inside the box until dark and had Mom worried sick. From that point on, we knew we couldn't trust him, but he had persuading ways. He always made us think we had to do dumb things to have fun.

"Hell with him, let's smoke 'em," Tommy said.

I tossed the three cigarettes to Tommy. He picked two up, handed me one, and stuck the other in his pocket.

"Light me up," I said.

Tommy struck a match, and we lit both cigarettes with one flame. "Oh, they're smooth," I sputtered out as I coughed. Tommy coughed too.

"Yeah, super smooth...Huh, Viceroy. That's a new one," Tommy said as he looked at the side of his cigarette.

I pulled in a drag and tried to make a smoke ring but failed. Oz could make great smoke rings. Experience will do that though.

"Man, I'm freezing. What are we going to do with Oz's cigarette?" asked Tommy.

"Save it; we'll have it later if he doesn't come."

"This Viceroy is making me dizzy," Tommy whispered.

"We must be smoking them right if we're getting dizzy," I assured him. "Good thing these aren't cigars. My Grandpa said that if a kid smokes a cigar, he better have his pant legs tied off, so when he craps his pants it won't SPLATTER all over the floor."

"Maybe we should give one to Oz," Tommy said laughing. "That would be great. Here, Oz…smoke this," he said as he held out his cigarette and then stuck his tongue between his lips to make a sound like he was passing gas. "Pbbbbbbb," we were both laughing so hard we were having a tough time not burning ourselves.

Tommy held up his weed and flicked off the orange glow with the middle finger of his other hand. "Ya done?" he asked.

"Yeah, let's get out of here," I said as I crushed the butt with my foot.

Tommy crawled out of the hole, and I followed close behind.

"Hey! Where you guys going?" Oz said while standing on the porch with his hands on his hips.

"We're freezing," Tommy responded with his arms folded together and his legs marching in place to stay warm, "We're going home."

"Yeah, see ya later," I added turning toward my house.

"What about the smokes?"

"We smoked 'em. See ya," Tommy said trying to get away.

"You what?"

"Oh, here is yours," Tommy said to Oz as he pulled the cigarette out of his pocket. He handed it to him in two pieces. Oz looked at it and knocked it out of his open palm. In the same motion, he pushed Tommy with one hand. Tommy landed on his back, but the deep snow broke his fall. Tommy looked up from the ground with his stocking cap slightly off from the jolt.

"What did you do that for?" I asked cautiously, knowing I could get the same treatment. I wasn't very big, but I was willing to take a beating for Tommy.

"You little assholes are in deep shit," Oz said angrily.

"What are you talking about?" I asked.

"You guys are screwed," he continued, "don't you know you have to light a Viceroy with a blue-tip match or you will be pissing blue for a week?" Oz was swearing with fury, but this time it wasn't funny.

"Really?" asked Tommy.

"Don't listen to him. He's full of shit," I said with confidence.

"Full of shit, huh? You'll see. I hope you don't wet the bed tonight, Tommy," Oz said sympathetically, "just think your very own Rock Lake right in your bed."

"Knock it off," I said, trying to reassure Tommy, but having some doubt in my own mind.

"My mom is going to be so mad," Tommy said with a worried look.

"Come on, Tommy," I said while helping him up. We turned away from Oz and started to head toward my home. I thought to myself, *He can't be telling the truth; he never does.*

As we crossed the street, Oz yelled, "You stupid morphodites! Don't try to take a piss now. It takes a few hours to kick in!" I just shook my head.

"I knew we should have waited for him," Tommy said.

"Yeah, no kidding."

"Let's just ask your mom to see if he's right," Tommy suggested.

"Yeah, Tommy. Sure. Hey Mom, we were smoking some Viceroys, and we didn't use the right matches. Are we going to piss blue now? Great idea, Tommy," I said sarcastically.

"Well, let's ask Chris then."

"Now you're thinking."

We stamped the snow off our feet and entered my house. The warmth felt good, and I could smell supper cooking. Mom was stirring something on the stove as she looked up and said, "We're going to eat in about fifteen minutes."

"Okay...Where's Chris?" I asked.

"Upstairs. Tell him supper will be ready soon," she answered.

"Alright," I said. I motioned Tommy with my head. We took the stairs two at a time. We walked down the hall to Chris's bedroom like it was the most important meeting of our lives. We didn't even take time to take our coats off. I looked over my shoulder, and Tommy has a real worried look pasted on his face.

I nodded at Tommy and said, "Chris will know." He just nodded back.

As we walked through the door, Chris looked up. There were models all over his room, mostly cars and a few planes. One big aircraft carrier that took him weeks to create sat all alone. That was his biggest accomplishment so far. He was holding onto a tweezers, and we could see that he had a small model piece in it. He looked back down and carefully glued the piece to the engine of the car he was building. I looked at the box and could see that it was a '57 Chevy.

"What are you two up to?" Chris asked, as he searched for another piece.

For an older brother, Chris was always willing to help. He wasn't like some older brothers that I have seen. Some of my friends stayed away from their older brothers just to avoid a beating. Chris was not like that at all.

"Ask him," Tommy said, pushing me a bit from behind.

"Ask me what?" Chris said.

I started laying out the whole story to Chris while Tommy interrupted with unnecessary details. Chris continued to glue small, grey pieces of an engine together. I almost thought he was not listening until I got to the pissing blue part. He suddenly looked up and a small smile creased his lips as though the story finally captured his attention.

When I finished, Tommy quickly asked, "Well...is that true? Is Oz telling the truth?"

Chris sat back in his chair with his arms folded in front of himself. He shook his head and said, "I gotta admit, the kid's a wizard."

"It's true then? Hey wait," Tommy looked like a light bulb just came on in his head, "maybe that's why they call him Oz!"

Chris just gave him this blank stare and said, "Huh? Yeah... right. . .anyway. . ." Chris was still trying to process Tommy's statement, and then he looked right at Tommy and asked, "Haven't you ever been to someone's house and when you go to take a leak the water in the toilet is blue?"

"Yeah, yeah! Oh crap, it is true then?" Tommy asked.

"Whose house has blue water?" Chris fired back.

"Peter's! His old man smokes Viceroy's?" Tommy asked with a confused look on his face.

At first, I didn't know where Chris was going with this, but then it dawned on me that he was stringing Tommy along. Chris continued with, "NO! He doesn't smoke. No one in their family smokes."

"Then how come they're pissing blue?"

"They're not! There's a blue deodorizer in their water tank."

"A what?"

"Forget it," Chris said waving his hand, "if Oz ever had to tell the truth, it would kill him. Don't tell me you guys believed that crap! Do I have to remind you that this is the kid that steals milk money from porches and takes a carrot out of a snowman's head and places it below its waist? When are you guys ever going to learn?" Chris said, smiling and nodding his head at the same time.

"Well, we weren't sure," I said.

"I have a plan that will get that weasel back," Chris said. "This is what we'll do..."

After supper, I told my mom that I was going over to Tommy's house, as I sped towards the door.

"Okay, be home by eight," she said.

"Alright," I said.

It was dark outside, so it wouldn't take long to complete the plan that Chris laid out to me. Tommy was nowhere in sight, so I had to do the deed by myself. Thank God I hadn't taken a leak since noon. My bladder was ready to burst. Chris told me to drink a few extra glasses of water for supper, but I think I over did it.

The next morning, as Eddie and I ate breakfast, Mom walked into the kitchen and said casually, "Oz's mom called this morning and wanted to know if any of you guys were out late last night."

Mom knew I was the only one out, but she acted like she forgot. Last night in bed, I told Eddie what I had done, so he knew. I felt Eddie kicking me under the table. I stared into my Sugar Frosted Flakes and listened as my mom continued. I sneaked a quick look at Eddie, and he grabbed the box of Sugar Crisp and was looking at the side of the box like he was actually going to read the ingredients. I could see a slight smile grow on his face. I was thinking, *Oh God, I can't look at him. I* ***will*** *start laughing.*

"A funny thing happened over there," she said, "seems someone peed in their front yard."

I couldn't even look at Eddie because he was starting to snicker. I knew at this point Mom knew who did it, but she also knew Oz's history and probably figured he had it coming. "Not only did someone pee in their yard, but he spelled something in the snow."

Eddie's head rose and his face had a look of confusion. I told him what I had done, but I left out one small detail. Eddie had to ask, "What did it say?"

"Strangest thing," Mom said.

"WHAT?" Eddie asked with curiosity.

Mom looked right at me and said, "It said V I C E R O Y!"

12

We were weaving through the peaks and valleys of the bluffs; the music was barely audible, but I was able to recognize the song, and I liked it. I reached for the radio to turn it up, and Mary slapped my hand. I knew she was messing with me which was okay. I gave her a finger in the ribs to acknowledge her sign of play. She was in the middle seat, and she was in charge of the radio. That had always been the rule in our car. Being seated in the middle had to have some benefits. I think Mom laid out that law many years ago when someone complained. Mom was the world's best negotiator and could solve a dilemma in minutes. Mary handled the volume button like she was trying to open a safe. She spun it a little to the left, a little to the right, to the left one more time. BINGO. "Shambala" from Three Dog Night came in crystal clear. With one mission accomplished, she began another one. She started fishing around inside a crumpled-up paper bag that looked like she had carried it with her for months. She was briskly moving the articles inside. Her dark brown, shoulder-length hair was suspended on the sides of her head. It hung like a curtain, not allowing me to see her face. I watched her as she finally found what she was looking for. She pulled out a pack of Wrigley's Doublemint. It was already open, and she offered me a piece, by just holding the pack up. One piece was already sticking up higher than the others. I grabbed it, and she pulled out two more pieces. She handed one to Mom and with her piece she used her teeth to pull the inside, silver sleeve out of the outer green wrapper. She crumpled up both pieces of paper and threw them inside the bag. I took the bag from her hands and looked inside. It was full of empty wrappers of candy, gum, and new tissues.

"No wonder you can't find anything in there," I said.

"I know. I was going to throw all this junk away before we left, but I forgot," she said.

I handed the bag back to her, and she continued to search for something else. Mary was one of a kind. She had more spunk and attitude than any one of my brothers. She knew more about sports than any girl I knew. She was the first one in front of the TV on Sunday to watch Packer games. She not only knew the names of all the Packers, she also knew the names of all the players on the other teams. Eddie and I had small, plastic football helmets that we used to teach her the teams. She must have been all of three when we quizzed her for the first time. We had three hours to burn when we were in the back of our station wagon traveling to south Chicago to see our Grandpa and cousins. We used that opportunity to show her a helmet and ask her which team it was. It didn't take her long to learn the teams. The only two she had trouble with were the Vikings and Falcons. She called them the Fikings and the Valcons. It was close enough, so we let her slide with her interpretation. It got to the point where she would intentionally say those names just to hear our reaction. She was always interested in sports, having four older brothers might have something to do with that. She had the misfortune of being the only girl on the block other than Claudia. The neighborhood was thick with boys, and then there was Mary. As she got a little older, she wanted to play baseball and football with the rest of us kids, so we did let her play a few football games. Her speed kept us from really getting a good tackle on her. Mary's strength was not playing sports with the neighborhood boys; it was knowledge of the game. A bunch of kids would be hashing out the problems of the Packers, and Mary would chime in with a remark that made us realize she was doing her homework.

She was always my biggest fan, no matter what sport I was playing. She attended most of my games and matches and always had an analytical comment regarding the events that had happened. Sportscasters were all men, so I wondered what she was going to do with her future, but I knew she would figure it out.

Looking out the window of the car and seeing the trees fly behind us, made me finally realize that I would not be on the return trip. I now understood why my mom was taking the long way. I took a deep breath and tried to capture the moment. Mary must have seen the look in my eyes, and she started to talk about the highlights of our past.

"Hey Pat, remember when Eddie buried me up to my neck in dirt and then put the bushel basket over my head? Next, he told you and Mom to come outside to see the odd- looking bug he caught?"

"Jesus Christ, I thought I was going to have a heart attack," said Mom, shaking her head. "When I tipped that basket over and saw nothing but your head, I didn't know if I was going to faint or go blind. I wanted to brain you kids for scaring the crap out of me." Just to hear Mom's reaction was enough to make Mary and I both laugh hysterically. Mom was laughing right along with us. Her laugh was always accompanied with a coughing fit. Smoking made sure of that.

"Pat, how about the time you and Eddie dressed up like elves and put bent hangers in your socks to make it look like your shoes were curled up and then stood outside the window so Mary could see you on Christmas Eve?"

"I believe that was your idea because Mary was being naughty and you wanted to put a scare into her," I said.

Mary held out her arms like she was trying to stop a train and said, "Wait a minute! You mean that was you and Eddie?" Mom nearly spit out her cigarette with that remark. Half of the small, orange glowing ember flew in multiple directions as she tried to contain her laughter. She padded a few ashes that landed on her lap.

"I need a bathroom break; let's pull off and recharge," Mom said.

This time I was in agreement with her. I knew we would be there soon and was wondering if we could even take a longer route. The longer, the better, I thought. Mom parked the car and gave Mary and me a buck. I stuck the dollar in my pocket, and Mary went inside the gas station to get supplies to fill her paper bag. I looked inside the car and saw the bag sitting on the front seat. I knew she wouldn't actually empty it before we left. The car looked bare. I looked at the seats and had a vision of our whole family inside. It would have been great if all of us could have shared this trip as well as the stories. I was really hoping that my dad would have joined us, but he rarely did anything that changed his routine. Once, we begged him for weeks to take us to our first Brewers game. We were so relentless, and I think my mom was sick of hearing us pester him, so much that she joined in too.

"Come on, Bob, let's go to a game," she said, "Please."

Finally, he couldn't stand it anymore, so he stood up from his Lazyboy and said, "Jesus Christ, that's enough, we'll go." The special feeling of going to the game was lost with that attitude. The whole time there, I felt like we were putting him through torture. He never complained, but he never said he was enjoying himself either until we were leaving the parking lot to go home. "That was fun," he said in a low voice, like he was ashamed to admit it. No one said a word.

Only once, he spent quality time with me and me alone. The Cub Scouts had a camping trip, and everyone in my den was going, so I think he felt some kind of obligation…

As we turned out of the campgrounds and proceeded back home, I got on my knees and spun around on the front seat of the car. I looked out of the rear window and saw the Camp Indian Trails sign fade in the distance. After a few minutes, Dad asked, "What are you looking at?" I didn't know what to say. The feeling of fulfillment that held me only yesterday was still alive. It compared to a perfect paper in school. I felt proud for some reason.

The calendar was full of special summer events in the summer of '64, but none of those would ever measure up to the two days I spent with my dad. As we finished packing up the car, Dad reminded me that the Scout's Motto was, "Always be prepared." I knew the motto, but it made me feel better that he knew it also. Suddenly, I realized that this weekend was going to be with my dad, and that he was someone I really didn't know very well. Dad kept to himself and very rarely opened up.

The only time that happened was when the brandy was talking for him and then you couldn't shut him up. I was more concerned about how he was going to handle the weekend than what kind of time I was going to have. Our conversation was light on the way to camp. We talked about my ball team, the coach, and how I liked playing shortstop. He also gave me a few tips on fielding. We were just starting to make a connection when the Camp Indian Trails sign came into sight, and we both said it together laughing over the coincidence. As we unloaded the station wagon, Dad searched for the ideal place to set camp, and he even asked me for my approval. It made me feel important. When I agreed the sight was perfect, we arranged everything in our tent together. The camp was littered with boys and dads, and it was beginning to transform into a canvas village.

A whistle blew in the distance, and a camp leader approached to explain our first activity. I didn't feel like I was marine Gomer Pyle, but the leader looked and sounded a lot like Sergeant Carter. "Gentleman, your first duty is to advance forward and withdraw a satchel from this box."

I was thinking, *What the heck is a satchel?*

"Your objective is to find physical evidence of nature." In the distance a small hand flew up in the air. The leader/sergeant had his hands behind his back as he spoke. He pointed to the young scout that had his hand raised and said, "Yes?"

"Um, what's a zatchel?" A few sporadic laughs came from the cluster of campers, but Sergeant Carter put a quick stop to that. He held up his hand quickly to squelch any humor.

"Good question, young man," he said. "Proceed ahead and I will show you." We all walked toward the sergeant. He was handing out small leather bags. When everyone had one, he continued his announcement. He held the leather bag in the air and said, "Satchel! With an **S.** Take these satchels and collect leaves, pine needles, insects, and any objects that fall within these grounds. Do NOT hurt or harm anything for the simple reason of collection!" Another small hand shot into the air. Once again he pointed toward the scout. "Yes?"

"What if we find a dead bird or something?" Again, more laughter occurred from the masses.

"Well, young man, if you find a dead bird...or something, if you want to put *that* inside your satchel and carry it around with you, that's your decision. If you find something that is too big to put inside your satchel, let's say... a dead bear or deer; you just let me know and we will have it for dinner!" The kids and the fathers liked that. All kinds of comments were created from that remark.

The sergeant talked over the commotion: "Now, commence to collect and meet me at the mess hall at fourteen hundred hours."

I looked up at Dad, and before I could say a word, he said, "Two o'clock." I just nodded.

During our walk, we picked up various things like pinecones, acorns, leaves, and a dead monarch butterfly.

When I saw the butterfly lying in the grass, I ran to it and yelled, "Hey look!"

Dad said, "Bring it over here." I carefully ran it over to him and laid it out in the palm of his hand. Dad lifted it and carefully placed it in the bag. "Good find, but don't tell the leader, we might be eating it for dinner." It was a funny statement, but somehow I thought it could happen. I asked what time it was and he said, "Almost two. We better get to the mess hall."

"Yeah."

We were walking through tall grass, and we could see the mess hall at the bottom of a hill. Dad suddenly veered right. He was walking with a purpose. I asked him where he was going and he said, "Come here a minute, Pat." I obeyed and followed the stepped- down grass he was trampling in his path. He stopped in front of me and was looking at a tree that was snapped off a few feet up from its base. He said, "What do you think happened here?"

"A storm?"

He looked around the surrounding area and said, "You're probably right by the looks of some of the other trees." There were larger trees with branches broken off. He pulled a pocket knife from his pocket and snapped out a blade.

"I didn't know you had a knife."

"I usually don't carry one. Look," he said, as he pointed to the center of the stump, "see the rings?"

"Yeah."

"Let's see how old this tree is."

He started to count the rings out loud with the tip of his knife. When he got to thirty-nine, he started to carve a letter by the ring. I watched trying to figure out what he was doing. After a minute, I could see a neatly cut *R* in the wood, and my curiosity couldn't hold back my question.

"What are you doing, Dad?"

"Just a second."

He wasn't finished, as he carefully worked on another letter. He blew off the small wood chips as he worked. He took his other hand and pushed off the bigger fragments. He finished the second letter and went back to the first to round out the top part of the *R*. "There," he said, as he cocked his head a bit to observe his work, "now it's your turn." He handed me the knife.

He pointed to the *RD* and said, "Robert Davis, thirty-nine."

"Oh, okay."

"Count the rings and put your initials there," he said.

I used the tip of the knife just like he did and counted to nine. It took me a little longer to get the *PD* just right, but it looked good. I found myself cocking my head just as he did to accept my work.

"There. Now when you're thirty-nine, and I'm ah…let's see…a hundred and something, we can come back out here and see if this is still here."

I was doing the math in my head when I realized he was trying to be funny. I finally laughed and said, "Yeah, a hundred and something."

"Come on; let's get going before they send a search party for us."

As we walked to the mess hall, I kept thinking that I was going to try to remember exactly where that tree was. I was going to come back just to see if it was still there when I was thirty-nine. As we walked, I looked back several times to take in the surroundings, trying to lock them in my memory.

My hunger was ringing with the sound of the mess hall dinner bell. As we approached the mess hall, I could see the Sergeant sitting by a picnic table. He was collecting all the items the scouts were bringing him. He would first ask them their name and then he received their satchels. He wrote their names on a piece of paper and then inserted it into the bag. His assistant was tying the end with a string so nothing would fall out. Someone from the door of the hall yelled that it was dinner time. The stream of scouts and dads flowed toward the hall. I soon found out why they called it the *mess hall.* It was obvious that the kitchen was a foreign place for the cooking staff. The hotdogs were like rubber, and the beans were burned. The comments from the dads were numerous and humorous.

"Hey Deano, did you lose the directions on how to boil water?" yelled one dad towards the kitchen. The dads in white aprons were visible through the large serving hole in the wall. One dad, it must have been Deano, just waved that comment off, but he must have said something back because there was a bit of laughter near the kitchen that I could not make out. Lemonade was the perfect description for our drinks. Lemons that needed help! It was so sour it made me pucker. To the cooks delight, the previous activities made us all hungry. My dad told me he had had worse food, but it would take him time to remember where. As we exited the mess hall, the Rock River was directly below us at the bottom of the hill.

"You want to go canoeing?" Dad asked.

"Sure!"

The grass we walked through to get to the river was freshly cut, and it smelled like summer. The river gave off a light trickling sound. The wind was calm, and the river barely had a ripple. As we walked down toward the river, Dad put his arm around me and asked me if I wanted the front or the back of the boat. It was the first time he had ever shown any kind of physical love toward me other than an occasional wink. The feeling overwhelmed me so that I felt a lump in my throat. I just swallowed hard. Dad noticed my face and pulled me a little closer saying, "Don't worry. We'll get lifejackets on." I wanted to freeze that moment in time. It would be a moment I would replay repeatedly in my mind many times in the future.

The evening approached with the excited anticipation of a bonfire and ghost stories. The huge fire, glowing in the center of the grounds, was the symbol of the energy we all had. We were all sitting on logs in a large circle. We were far enough away from it, but the heat of the fire kept my face warm. The sky was crystal clear, and the stars were as close as I'd ever seen them. The sound of slaps echoed in the night until a can of bug spray was relayed around the circle to ward off the mosquitoes. The pests hadn't had this much to eat since last year's feed. Once the can arrived at its original destination, the silhouette of a scout leader stood up and walked toward the center. As he got closer to the fire, it was clear that it was the Sergeant. He made some announcements and gave out verbal awards to scouts that found unusual items. My monarch was mentioned, and sure enough, someone did find a dead bird and brought it back with them. One of the dads spoke up and begged him not to put it in our breakfast. He quickly shot back that there wasn't enough for everyone, so he was going to eat it himself. Some songs were sung, and the ghost stories were told to conclude our evening. Multiple beams of light flashed through the blackness as our flashlights found our way back to camp. The sight of all those beams slashing the trees, ground, and sky made me think that we were in search of more than our camp, searching for a way to keep times like these forever.

Our tents appeared under the shadows of the tall pine trees illuminated by the light of the moon. The camp was soon filled with life, but the events of the day began to take its toll. One by one, scouts and dads began to disappear into the tents we called our home. The night seemed to last only minutes before the chirping crickets were replaced by the cawing of crows. The dew was heavy as we trudged toward the mess hall for our last meal. The food was the major discussion on the way. Many scouts and dads were glad to be going home to good food, while I was wishing the day wouldn't end. The cooks threw together sausage and scrambled eggs, and this time they got it right.

"Compliments to the cook," I heard one dad say. I saw Deano taking a short bow. He may have lost his recipe for boiling water, but he had the sausage and egg recipe mastered. One day of experience in the kitchen did these dads a lot of good. I asked my dad why he didn't volunteer to cook since he was a baker and could make anything. He told me that he needed a break from that.

"Besides," he said, "I wanted to spend time with you, not next to a hot oven." As we finished eating, the Sergeant got everyone's attention.

He was holding his two arms straight out with his palms down trying to calm the place down. The chatter in the room diminished to a whisper. In a rather hoarse voice, he said, "Gentleman, I want to take this time for a few announcements. First of all, I know many of you have complained about the food we had yesterday, but I believe today's breakfast made up for that." He started to applaud and the rest of the room followed his lead. "It's not easy to feed this many people, and if I have any volunteers to take their places for next year, I will need a show of hands." He raised his hand halfway up to show us how to do it. He scanned the crowd to see no hands in the air. He looked toward the kitchen and said, "Well Deano, looks likes the job is yours next year."

Deano was standing in the kitchen, and we could see him through the opening of the wall. A cigarette was hanging from his lip. He pulled the butt from his mouth and leaned on the counter toward the crowd and said, "I gladly accept the nomination as chief cook and bottle washer next year."

The Sergeant smiled and shot back, "The contract is in my car. I'll need you to sign it before you change your mind. Next, I'd like to say that this is the first year we had campers for a whole weekend and no major illnesses or injuries were reported other than that poor dead bird. The only mention of illness was shortly after yesterday's dinner, and the outhouses accommodated us well. In closing, I hope all of you had a good time and that you will be back with us again next year. Have a safe trip home and thanks for coming!"

...I could hear my dad talking, but it was in the distance. His voice was getting louder, so I turned to him as I kneeled on the front seat of the car.

"Pat, what are you looking for?"

What I was looking for could not be seen. I was looking to lock in a memory that I wanted to take with me forever. I turned and faced the road and the feeling of pride again came over me.

"You Okay?" Dad asked.

"I'm fine."

I thought about the small sign of affection he had given me by the river. The thought that he couldn't give me that on a regular basis really didn't bother me. The fact that he showed me *once* was proof that it had always been there, but it was hidden by an outer crust that was hard to crack. That small spark of love ignited an eternal flame that I continue to carry with me. A flame not fueled by affection but by memory. It wasn't much, but it was something that no one could ever take away from me. The moment by the river was not only the best part of the weekend, but the best memory I ever had with my dad.

13

I saw that we were approaching a city, and I asked where we were. No one answered, probably because the radio was somewhat loud. The Staple Singers were just ending their song, an appropriate song at that. "I'll Take You There" was the name of it. I reached to turn the radio down, and I could see Mary's hand come up. She was ready to swat me, so I just pointed to the knob and gave her the turning motion to turn it down. She turned the volume down and said, "LaCrosse. That's where we are, your new home."

"We're here already?" I asked.

"Afraid so," Mom said.

The radio was set to a whisper, and yet I could hear the next song as clear as a bell. "Too Late to Turn Back Now" was going into the chorus for the second time. *How fitting, I* thought. I was about to ask Mary to turn it up, but before I got two words out, she quickly said, "Cornelius Brothers and Sister Rose."

"I know who sings it; just turn it up a bit."

It was a game we played. A song would come on, and we quizzed each other on who sang it. Mary was the best at it. I knew many artists, but I think she had a personal book to log in every song ever written. It was hard to stump her, and many times she would deliberately say the wrong artist. Then before I could correct her, she would correct herself. She was pretty much a tease, but that came honestly. Teasing in our family was a way of life. We learned at an early age that if you couldn't take teasing, you may as well stay in your room all day. It was done in good nature though and rarely mean-spirited. Mom would not allow that. She always had her ear to the banter and a simple, "That's enough," would end any further hurting words. She couldn't stop us from fighting though. Bob and Chris did that, and Eddie and I followed suit. It was always over something stupid. Usually someone would "borrow" some thing from someone else. The problem was that the thing "borrowed" was never returned until you saw it in their room. That's when the arguments and fights ensued.

Many times when I went to confession, I had to make stuff up just to condone going there. Not that I was saint or anything, but contrary to many beliefs, Catholics don't walk out of the confessional with the idea that they were totally resolved and can begin to plot their next bank heist. Fighting with Eddie was something I didn't have to fabricate. I can only speak for myself, but confession made me a better person.

Eddie and I really didn't fight a lot, but when we did, it wasn't pretty. Many times Mom would let it go as long as she could stand it. When she had had enough, she would storm the room and scream at us. If there was one thing she hated, it was us fighting, and we knew it. It totally broke her down to see two of her own sons fighting. To see Mom's hurt face after we had had a brawl was enough to think real hard next time we wanted a piece of each other.

"That was 'Your Mama Don't Dance' by Loggins and Messina. 'We're an American Band' by Grand Funk Railroad coming up next and then Elton John singing about 'Daniel' here on 89 WLS in Chicago. Be sure to join us every morning as Fred Winston gets you to work with today's hits. Stay with us, because we'll be back in a few minutes, right after these important messages."

A commercial started, and Mary turned the radio down a little as we started to enter the city of LaCrosse.

"Which streets are we supposed to turn on?" Mom asked.

Before answering, I was waiting to see what street we were on. I was looking at the pamphlet that was sent to me. It had a detailed map laid out starting from Madison, and I was trying to figure out which way was the easiest way, coming in from the east. "When you come to this next street, take a left," I told Mom.

"Let's get some lunch before we go to the dorm. How does that sound?" Mom asked.

"That's fine."

"I feel like pizza," said Mary.

I put my hand on top of Mary's head and squeezed her scalp saying, "Yeah, you do feel like pizza."

"Shut up," she said as she leaned into my shoulder.

"Let's have a good meal; you'll have plenty of pizza in the next few months," Mom suggested.

"Okay," I said.

We pulled into a diner that advertised: "HOME COOKED FOOD."

The windows of the diner were fogged up from the cold. It was close to zero, and there was a slight breeze as we exited the car. I immediately zipped up my coat, even though I only had a few feet to walk before getting warm. Mary had her hands jammed into her pockets, and she walked ahead of Mom and me. Her hair blew in the breeze. She was about to open the door when a man came out and held it open for us. Mary didn't miss a stride and proceeded inside. I took the door from the man, thanked him, and held it open for Mom. She was lagging behind after retrieving her purse from the car. She was holding her chiffon scarf around her chin, making sure it wouldn't blow away. She took quick, short steps as she entered the diner. I followed behind her, and we were met by a waitress. She had a light blue uniform on along with a red sweater that was open in the front. I could see that she had a large pocket, waist level where she kept her pad. A pencil stuck out of her hair next to her ear. Her nametag said Betty.

"Just three?" she asked.

"Yup," I said.

"Would you like a booth, or do you want to sit at the counter?"

Mom answered before I could even think of the options, "We'll take a booth."

"Right this way."

We followed Betty to an open booth where Mary scooted in first, and I sat next to her; Mom sat across from us. We took off our coats and laid them behind us. Betty asked us if we wanted anything to drink. Mom ordered coffee, and Mary and I each wanted a Coke. We pulled the menus out from behind the metal rack that held the salt, pepper, and napkins. The diner was crowded, and by the sounds of the conversations around us, most of the people knew each other. Next to our booth, two men were sitting at a table. One was a soldier in uniform, the other a young man with shoulder length hair. The soldier was doing most of the talking, and the young man was leaning forward with his elbows on the table and his hands folded in front of him. He was listening and bobbing his head in agreement. I immediately thought of my two brothers and how different their paths were during the Vietnam War…

The Civil War had been over for more than a hundred years. Our family chose to celebrate its memory by having our very own war. There was no loss of life, flesh wounds, or overtaking of strategic territory. There was really no loss at all in comparison to the real horrors of the "War Between the States." However, there were scars that would take years to heal.

The year was 1968, and I had just turned thirteen. My oldest brother, Bob, had been out of school for three years. His athletic accomplishments were still felt in the halls and trophy cases of Lake Mills High School. He was an outstanding football player and also excelled in track. He was built to take punishment and was ready to take anyone on, anyone that dared to. No one or no thing could intimidate him. He was the popular, letter jacket wearing, All American jock.

Chris was formed from a totally different mold. He was tall, lean, and quiet. Although very athletic, golf was his game. It reflected his passive personality. He found out early that he couldn't measure up to his brother in football, or any other sport in which Bob was involved. The only resemblance Chris had with *him* was his last name. As they matured, they developed wings of independence. One flew as a hawk, the other as a dove.

In our family, there was very little interest in the Vietnam War until Bob received his lottery number, a two digit number that had more meaning than its sum. It was just a matter of time before *the letter* arrived. The courier gave specific directions of where to partake in a physical for the Armed Forces. He accepted his duty as expected, and once again, he was the pride of the family. He breezed through his basic training and eagerly took on every challenge. The next option the Army presented to him needed some thought. He had to decide if he wanted to sign on for an additional year with the chance of becoming a part of the prestigious "Special Forces". As independent as he was, Bob surprisingly asked Dad for advice. Dad served in the Army-Air Force in World War II, so naturally he told him to, "*Go for it.*" As the patriotic song of the 60's went,

"*One hundred men will test today, but only three are the Green Beret.*" Bob became one of those three. He was the ultimate-fighting machine. The U.S. Army loved his type. He was smart, cunning, agile, and most importantly, obedient. Pictures, certificates, and documents hung throughout the house while he completed everything with excellence. Airborne, hand-to-hand combat and sharp shooting qualified him as an expert. No one was more proud than Dad.

Chris, however, was again lost in the shadow of his older brother. He didn't need Vietnam to fight a battle. He had already engaged himself in his own private war. Chris was not only the poster child for the "peace sign," but his convictions were solid. With his shoulder-length hair, beard, and passive heart, he was a hippie in every sense of the word. His draft notice was the seed that grew hard feelings like an uncontrollable weed. Chris did not run away to Canada. He stood tall in front of the Military Board and explained his simple beliefs, "I can not and I will not kill anyone. No matter who tells me to do it," he stated.

I loved both brothers, and I was not about to take sides. My dad's military history gave him little choice as to what side he was to take. The heat from the napalm being dropped in the jungles of Vietnam matched the daily arguments Chris had with Dad. Standing up for his beliefs took its toll. With the label as a Conscientious Objector, he lost his privilege of living at home. Dad made that judgment. Chris was given a two year term working for the United States Government. This consisted of working for minimum wage at a day care center in Madison. His red Ford Falcon, with the back seat torn out (for more room), was to be his traveling home for the next two years. He gladly shared his space with his dog, Bromo.

The war tore my brothers out of the house in two different directions. Bob's direction was one for the love of his country; Chris's was for the love of life itself. Who was right and who was wrong? There had to be an answer somewhere. Our country's history leaned very heavily toward the war, and my father backed that belief daily. The college demonstrations made the issue even more difficult, and I knew that I would have to make a decision when I was drafted. Fortunately, that time never came because the draft ended along with the war. But, the question still remained. Who was right and who was wrong?

The government took care of my brothers in very different ways. Their lifestyles were evidence of their care. In both cases they stood up for what they believed in. Bob came home to a pat on the back and a "*Very well done!*" while Chris was the unwanted dog left on the doorstep. I loved them both, but was taught to respect a soldier that fights for the freedom of his country. I tried to convince myself that the soldier's choice was the correct one. Logically, I accepted that theory, but my heart just wouldn't let the issue die.

My questions were answered in the discovery of an old photograph. A lone picture that was tucked away and somewhat forgotten. It was one that I showed quite frequently as I grew up. I displayed it proudly many times to anyone that bragged about their family. The corners were turned and bent, and the picture itself was wrinkled almost beyond recognition from making the trip from my back pocket to my palm. The second it made its appearance, it brought back warm memories of days gone by and a feeling of whole love that filled my heart. All my friends talked about the athletic accomplishments of Bob and how lucky I was to have him as a brother. I had to agree; I was very proud of him. But I also knew something they didn't. I had another brother that meant enough to me, that I just had to have a picture of him with me all the time. This eighth grader in a plaid shirt possessed an innocent smile. His short hairstyle gave way to the "look" of 1961. I could only think of Chris and what a wonderful brother he was. Being seven years younger, I must have been a pest. But never once did he make me believe it. When I would deliberately step on the squeaking hallway board outside his bedroom door to wake him up, it never seemed to bother him. I didn't care what I did during the day as long as he did it with me. We played board games, baseball, and football. He took me to the carnival, movies, and taught me how to throw a knuckleball and play poker at age five. He coached my little league teams, drew treasure hunts throughout the house, and we wrestled upstairs with the mattresses on the floor. Many times the "roughhousing" made me cry, and I descended the stairs to tell my mom my woes. Her solution was a simple one: "Just don't go back up there," she'd say. That suggestion was totally unrealistic. I just had to be with him. The joy of being with Chris was worth the bumps and bruises. He didn't do things with me because of responsibility. He did it because he enjoyed being with me. The photo was a reminder of what a vested relationship meant, and it didn't matter what I was "supposed" to believe in. I loved this brother society had come to frown upon.

Through all of this, never once, did either brother condemn the other for their choices. They matured with their experience and welcomed each other home. Their mutual respect was very evident. Time took care of any hard feelings Dad had for Chris, and they grew into a father/son relationship the way it should have been.

Although the feelings for each of my brothers are different, my love for them remains the same. I'm proud to say, "We are brothers." They stood up for what they believed in, and their example made me a better person. My collection of photos through the years have been many, but few bring as much emotion and love as the one I held in my pocket many years ago.

The two men at the diner got up, and the soldier left a tip. The young man went to the counter to pay. I instinctively reached for my wallet to see if I still had that photo of Chris. I couldn't remember the last time I looked at it. I went through my whole wallet and couldn't find it. I remember a few months back getting a new wallet and going through some of the items I carried with me for the last few years. I did throw away some insignificant papers that no longer had any use to me, but I know for sure that photo would not have been one of them. I must have put that picture in my drawer at home. It was probably there, but it still bothered me that I didn't have it with me, and I couldn't recall where it was.

"What'll ya have?" Betty said.

"What do you want kids?" Mom asked.

Mary said, "I'll have the hamburger with the works and fries."

"Okay, and you sir?" asked Betty.

"I'll have the same with fried onions," I said.

"Ma'am?" Betty asked as she looked over her glasses at my mom.

"I'll have the special," Mom said as she continued to scan the menu.

"Meatloaf it is," Betty replied.

Betty finished writing on her pad and then walked to the kitchen to place our order.

14

We finished our lunch, and Betty promptly asked us if we wanted dessert. As I sat there, I was trying to think if I had ever eaten at a restaurant with just my sister and Mom. I'm convinced the answer to that was no. Out of nowhere, my mom asked us if we wanted pie.

"Sure," I said.

Mom looked at Mary and said, "How about you, Hon?"

I looked at Betty and said, "Mary hates pie; she doesn't want any."

Betty quickly said, "Okay, no pie for Mary." Then she gave a wink and let out a small laugh, knowing I was kidding.

Mary was giving me the wide-eyed look like she was about to strangle me. She had a smile on her face, so I knew she wasn't too upset. Mary looked at Betty and said, "I'll try the cherry." Mom and I ordered the blueberry.

"I wonder if the pie is going to be as good as Dad makes?" Mom asked. We all had our mouths full when we looked at each other and decided it didn't come close. A strange feeling crept into me as we got closer to finishing our dessert. It dawned on me that in less than an hour I would be in an unfamiliar place with no family or friends around. I was beginning to have doubts about my choice of going to college in a city that was so far away. Sure, it was only 160 miles from home, but since my travels were limited, to me it was the other side of the world. I tried to regain the excited feeling I had when I decided that being away was going to be fun, but I couldn't muster that thought.

"We should probably get you to the dorm before they lock you out," Mom said.

"Yeah, then you'll have to come back home with us," Mary added.

Betty dropped off the bill and wished us a good day. Mom dug in her purse and laid out a tip. She gathered her coat from behind her and put it on while Mary and I did the same. Mary pulled her paper bag from her pocket and started rummaging around in it again. She found what she was looking for and popped a piece of candy in her mouth. "Want a piece?" she asked me.

"No thanks," I said, "I know Christmas is a long way away, but maybe with a little luck, I can buy you what you really need."

"What?" she asked.

"A brand-new paper bag."

Without even a smile, she said, "Why bother this one is still good. Don't waste your money." I laughed at her response. It was pretty hard to put one over on Mary unless you dressed up like an elf.

As we got into the car, I retrieved my small map and gave directions to Mom. After a few miles and several turns, we arrived at the dormitory. Parents and kids were carrying boxes into the dorm. I felt like I didn't have enough with me. All I had was one suitcase. It made me feel better when I thought it would be less to bring home when the semester ended. We entered the lobby of the dorm and talked to the advisor who looked up my name and instructed me that my room was on the third floor. We walked single file up the stairs in search of my next home. When I found my room, I discovered that the door was wide open. I could see that my roommate was already moved in, but he was no where in sight. I threw my suitcase on my bed and opened it. I turned around and Mom said, "Well Hon, we really should be going."

"Yeah, I guess so," I said.

As I hugged Mary goodbye, I thought about how much she meant to me, and that I should have hugged her a lot more while we were growing up. By the look in her eyes, she was going to miss me too. I could see tears in her eyes as she said, "I have something for you, but don't open it until we leave. Okay?"

"Okay."

She pulled out her crumpled up paper bag and gave it to me.

I looked at her like she was giving me her prized possession. "Don't worry, I got a new one at the last gas station," she said. She pulled out a new, folded bag just to show me.

"Come home when you can," she said.

"I will."

I looked at Mom and said, "Thanks for driving me up here."

"You're welcome. Give us a call once in a while; let us know how things are going."

"Alright."

She hugged me and said, "I'll talk to you soon."

Mom turned and scanned the room looking for Mary, but she was already in the hallway. She had her new bag open and was pulling pieces of candy out of her pockets and dropping them into it. I thought, "*That poor bag doesn't have any idea what it's going to endure.*" They walked down the hallway, and they were almost to the stairs when Mary turned and gave me one last wave. I returned it, and they were gone.

I walked to the window of my room and looked outside. I could see people continuing to haul their possessions into the dorm. Rather than using the sidewalks, they were walking through the snow to make a direct path to the doorway.

I went back to my bed, slid my suitcase over, and sat down. I was still holding Mary's paper bag in my hand. I opened the bag to see that she still hadn't thrown out the wrappers of her candy and gum. It was almost halfway full of just wrappers. I thought she was going to have the last laugh on me by giving me a gift of old gum and candy wrappers when I reached to the bottom of the bag and felt a rectangular object. I resurrected it from the floor of the bag. As I pulled it up through the paper debris, it reminded me of a show I saw where they were bringing a treasure up from the bottom of the ocean. I knew now why Mary never got rid of those wrappers. They concealed an envelope with Claudia's handwriting on the front. Claudia's penmanship was unmistakable. It was textbook and very neat. The only written word on the face of the envelope was *Pat*.

Claudia had been married for a little over a year, and she had moved to a nearby town. I hadn't been able to see her much, but for some reason seeing an envelope from her really didn't surprise me. She has always been one to remember a significant time in your life, and she frequently sent out cards to let you know she didn't forget. Just seeing the envelope with her handwriting on made me miss her. The object inside the envelope was smaller than the envelope itself. The envelope was not sealed; it was just folded so it wouldn't open. I unfolded the envelope and opened the flap. I pulled the contents from the envelope. The outside paper that was holding the harder object inside was a letter. It had the date on the outside: *January-1974.* Again, it was Claudia's writing and her typical way of always dating notes and cards. I opened the letter, and the object was surrounded by another piece of paper. I set the object on the bed and read the letter:

Pat,

Mary and I wanted to buy you something for college. We decided that this would be the best gift we could give you. Good luck!

Love always,
Claudia

I laid the letter on the bed and picked up the object. When I removed the paper, I could see that our Polaroid instamatic had captured some great moments of our family. The outside picture was of Eddie, Mary, and me sitting on the swing set. Eddie and I sported crew cuts, and Mary had her trademark braids. On the top of the photo was the partial date: JUL. 63. The date was printed on the picture when it was developed. There were separate pictures of Dad and Mom holding Mary, both: **APR . 63.** One photo captured my Grandpa and Chris painting the picket fence that surrounded our big backyard: **AUG . 63.** We probably bought the camera in 1963. That was evident by the dates. There was one of Bob standing in his prom tuxedo. There was no date on that one, but with some quick calculation, I came up with: Spring of 1964. Again, I saw the little league picture my mom had shown me this morning, and it puzzled me to think why this was only the second time I had seen it. The last one was Claudia standing outside with a plaid winter coat on. Her hood was tied around her head, showing only the bangs of her hair. There was no date on this one either, but there was half-melted snow on the ground. It was hard to tell if it was early winter or spring. Her hands were holding the chains of a swing as she smiled for the camera.

I had all the pictures laid out on the bed, and when I went to put the last one down, a small picture fell from my lap. It was much smaller than the rest. It landed face down. I reached down and picked it up. I turned it over. It was the picture of Chris that I carried all those years. Claudia must have taken it out of my drawer. She knew how much that picture meant to me. It not only gave me some relief of knowing where it was, but it dissolved much of the loneliness I was feeling five minutes earlier. Claudia and Mary were right; this was the best gift they could have given me. It was the gift that marked the beginning of my adult life and the end of a childhood, my childhood.

About The Author

Patrick G. Davis is the fourth child of a large Catholic family. He has a son, and a daughter, that are both college graduates. Patrick's initial job out of college was working for the Chicago and Northwestern Railroad. He was a fourth generation railroader. After 10 years of repairing, re-railing, and equipping train cars he looked for a more challenging career. He managed a resort in the summer and coached wrestling in the winter. He missed the work and the men he worked with at the railroad so he returned for a short time until he was laid off. He moved his wife and family to Arizona to pursue another railroad job, this time with Arizona Eastern Railway. After four years he moved again, back to where he called home; Wisconsin.

He always enjoyed writing, so with the encouragement from a teacher he put together a short story that is a testament to his love for his family and an appreciation to a very special childhood.

Printed in the United States
49929LVS00001BA/214-261

9 781425 927707